DARK PSYCHOLOGY AND MANIPULATION

Learn the hidden secrets of Dark Psychology to Persuade Analyze and Influence people. Became the Master of Persuasion and Manipulation

Margareth Bishop

By reading this document, the reader agrees that under no circumstances is the author responsible for any losses, direct or indirect, that are incurred as a result of the use of the information contained within this document, including, but not limited to, errors, omissions, or inaccuracies.

TABLE OF CONTENTS

INTRODUCTION

Manipulation has negative connotations for many. Nevertheless, it is required to accomplish targets, while using creativity to accomplish the same purposes, which seems to be only within the ability of a few.

You may use persuasion tactics for people to find reasons to purchase your product or service. If you want to develop long-term ties with your prospects or clients, manipulation, persuasion and mind control strategies are therefore more important.

Though manipulation sounds like a negative effect, most of us do it everyday. Likewise, most of us are affected subconsciously by external influences in our everyday actions and feelings. This characteristic tends to be an intrinsic part of our human decision- making process.

Moreover, manipulation can be healthy. Many corporations use constructive reinforcement to manipulate their clients. Manipulation can be very effective but only on a short-term basis does this work. Since manipulation or manipulating (now the preferred term) works only in the short-term, it is also important to focus on long- term consumer commitment.

Manipulative psychology places a mask on what we do, to improve productivity, and reduce the detection rate; these two go hand in hand when you think about it. If people do not know that we influence their thoughts and behaviors, then we are more likely to achieve the desired result.

One way we are continuously fooled is by "the crowd's wisdom." It's a little like telling the public at the Who Wants To Be A Millionaire contest. The hope is that the majority decision is the best in between.

We use manipulative psychology a lot on our kids, for example, when we tell them to eat greens or they won't be big and powerful.

This trick also works for older people, not just teenagers. It's perfect in an argument because you can huff and puff, saying things that practically compel someone to take your stance, even though they will only do so in the heat of the moment.

Perhaps my favorite method of using this form of psychological manipulation is to plant the seed of an idea into the mind of another. This needs some future planning but it's a treat. You say something in passing so that the minds of other people can pick it up and lock it away.

For the next few days or weeks, your mind will play with the idea and then unexpectedly, they will come up with the idea of which you first thought—except that they declare it as their own. This is not good, if your ego gets in the way, but it is great for getting your way because the other person was tricked at this point to believe it was their idea. Manipulative psychology attracts a poor welcome from the beginning. After all, the very words used to explain it mean you exploit something or someone and that is never a common choice with other people. Some questions need to be addressed.

The key ones are "what the heck is manipulative psychology?" and "should I use it?" In this GUIDE, I will do my best to answer these questions. If you can understand the concept of dark psychology and manipulation coupled with effective ways on how to recognize mind control techniques, emotional intelligence, body language to defend yourself from manipulation and persuasion and incorporate it in the way you market your business and relationship with people, the heights you achieve will not be limited.

Are you ready? Let's get started

CHAPTER 1

The Basics Of Dark Psychology

All of us have a dark side — the Jungian psychological shadow. This part of the self has dark urges, the negative instincts in us. This secret aspect of the self is good to know. There are signs here if you want to know how to recognize your dark side very well.

-- You know how your observations, assumptions and frustration at others represent your vulnerabilities, especially the psychological defense mechanism called projection colors, which affects how we think about others. Often, we add features to them which are our weaknesses.

– You understand the world's misery, bad, and suffering. Recognizing the evil around us can help us realize that evil is within us as well.

-- You know your words or actions will often convey anxiety and fear. Fear and anxiety are those emotions that the body or words convey as the heart races.

-- You know that your actions or deeds will often reflect resentment and envy. Jealousy and envy are rooted in egotism, which is very difficult to root out.

-- You know that your words and acts often convey covetousness and goodness.

Goodness and covetousness arise from our connection to this world's material and mental things.

-- You know your words often convey contempt and disdain. Contempt and disdain for others emerge from anger and hate-the result of not being able to cope positively with anger.

-- You are conscious of your anxieties and fears.

-- You are mindful of your jealousy and envious feelings.

-- You know the thoughts of covetousness.

-- You know the angry feelings. Knowing certain feelings will help you appreciate those acts that you find automatic (including saying something). Often we don't think we hurt people. We still feel deep inside, so unintentionally we hurt people. These unpleasant emotions are better known and healed with psychotherapies.

Knowing the dark side helps you to begin some changes in life. You will now know what ticks you off and you start to adapt accordingly. You will take a better approach to temptation and other attractions. Naturally, temptation doesn't fully vanish, but you are not left unprepared for such circumstances anymore.

The Benefits Of Meeting Our Dark Side

In psychology, the name "Shadow" (based on Carl Jung's theories) is given to a part of our self. This Shadow is our subconscious

instincts, our "dark side,"which is so much like a secret part of our self that we generally don't even want to reveal ourselves. We may not be aware of this, we may even be afraid to face it. But for the following advantages, it is best to visit our dark side.

• You can use your ingenuity and imagination to identify your own disowned portion. Some Shadow exploration exercises concentrate on drawing, mind mapping, and the like. Associations with our creative side will reinforce our link to this secret element of us all.

• You can restore any relationship for more truthful self-examination and direct contact. As some relationships are impaired by secret grudges, the more we see what we hide, the more we can understand certainties that are broken or are finished without an obvious cause.

• You will understand what you 'cast' to others, which then shapes some of our views on other individuals. We all prefer to see what we expect of ourselves in others. Instead of understanding the other person, we make "theories" on what the other person is based on what we know about us.

We might always start to think and ask "What will I do if I were him or her?" It's a reasonable question because you know that you ask him or her and don't use the thought to rashly evaluate your acts or thinking.

• You will start to be free of the remorse and the embarrassment we feel and our bad deeds, of course. We can see why the Catholic rite of confession has a psychological advantage. We must tackle our dark urges to get rid of them in any possible positive way.

• You can get rid of any unpleasant feelings that come unexpectedly during your everyday routine. We must reconcile ourselves with negative events and circumstances which unpredictably desolate us.

• Hopefully, you can gain true acceptance of yourself, a more full form of self-knowledge of who you are, and who you will be.

What We Need to Do to Explore Our Dark Side

Exploring our "dark side" or the Shadow (as Carl Jung's school called psychology) is a crucial step toward understanding our true selves. This dark side is our dark urges, dark inclinations, negative feelings and emotions, and the secret component that we often do not even reveal or consider to be ourselves. However, to discover the dark side, you must do the following.

• Close your mouth and open your heart. The essence of opening the heart is not only for opening the mind but for emotionally speaking. You must know your affections and emotions. Yeah, you do not want to feel them, but first of all, you know their presence because emotions exist inside you, whether you like them or not.

• Paradoxical embrace. An apparent contradiction is a paradox. We have to take it because once we enter the darkness, we can deal with those ideas-we've got a lot of evil in us but by nature, we're good. This line is a paradox and we must recognize it to understand it.

• Surrender your true "ideal self."

It is important to have models for good roles. But when we idealize too much or try to be better, we are still disappointed. Sacrifice these values and provide a practical approach to how to be nice. That does not mean that perfection does not exist, but we have to let go of frustration or we will be flawless in our eyes.

• Expand your consciousness.

Deep thought is required to measure our consciousness. Practice critical thought to learn more profound truths about your inner and real self.

• Drive slowly.

Do not hurry to self-awareness. Step slowly to accept the dark side. See what events the dark urges have exacerbated. Understand your remorse, your embarrassment and your dark, secret motives.

•   Continue to blame others. Now, these have major implications for your life and they can be profoundly relevant causal factors for your decisions. But, because of free will, your option is fine. Don't blame other people.

•   Transparency.

Own yourself. Know what you did and live with the repercussions of living as much as possible.

CHAPTER 2

Your Partner Is A "Mirror" That Shows Your "Dark Side"

Sooner or later, we'll all enter into a romantic relationship. Some relationships last a lifetime, while others crash faster. It is also true that our partners are just people with whom we want to do everything, whether it's a tour or hanging out. But they also represent our soul as we appear to open all our emotions to them. Both our mysteries and dilemmas lie naked before them. Ultimately, the solution is what we can do to fix them.

There is no problem when we share the light side with our friends. However, the real challenge is when we decide to expose our dark side. It is often assumed that we choose our mirror image unconsciously as a partner, who will do the same thing as we did initially.

To maintain a healthy relationship, we must let the other individual help us resolve our darker side's remorse and acts. This may cause some initial inhibitions in the early stages, but it is easier to address a problem than to make it worse. We should always take this kind of condition into account for a long-term objective.

The greatest issue in a relationship is that we want to portray ourselves as we are. The initial excitement for the relationship takes a back seat and the other one is not as they appeared at the first few meetings. Gradually we start to see the bad things more and more and get irritated.

Little by little, the relationship turns out to be a sour affair and we cannot wait long enough for it to end. But it is not appropriate to claim that it is time for serious maturity. We do have to note that everybody has a darker side, and the closest partner is the one who can help the other person cross the line. It is important to ask the right questions so that both individuals go in a positive direction.

When they start questioning the legitimacy of the things we do that can be amusing but are dangerous, the problem gets worse. Jesse Pink man and his love partner, Jane Margolis, in the popular Breaking Bad TV series may be the perfect example.

We can easily see that if an alcoholic Jane, who had lived soberly for almost a year and a half, unexpectedly goes back to doing drugs and things. This is the kind of relationship we can always stop and ask the right questions at the right time. This is the only way we can help our partner get rid of his/her character's dark side.

Often, one considers one another's attitude or behavior disturbing, so he or she has to try to figure out the real reason for it.

This is a long process, and both partners should approach it with great patience and caution so things do not become catastrophic for them. The reason for the relationship breaking down might arise from the slightest provocation.

Psychologists performed some studies to show the results of various kinds of experiences that could awaken the darker side and

ultimately allow us to get rid of them. They supported couples who continuously tried to break the ice when it comes to things that remained unknown, which may lead to problems.

Seminars helped many to tackle and overcome their challenges in the relationship. Psychologists have used simulations and developed scenarios to activate the character's depressive side and to use their immense psychological abilities to help couples get over them.

The biggest benefit of these encounters was that couples who attended multiple sessions about their insecurities found a lasting solution and never again repeated the same mistakes in their connections with their partner.

The best thing about consultations is to discover the reasons behind dark behaviors. You'll have a relaxed speech session to examine the issue in-depth and take further steps based on your preliminary results.

Therefore, all assessments and evaluations are personalized to each person. Couples are advised to use the strategies in the future if an issue reoccurs. The application of real-life cases is much more critical and psychologists are more than happy to give it.

Regardless of what the technical assistance tells you, it's always important to us to grasp the source of the problem and make it work. Psychologists recommend that couples should be adequately cooperative and often search for acts or interaction to demonstrate their positive emotions.

They also warn couples not to respond aggressively or to behave impulsively if their counterpart attempts to explain the effect of some dark behavior. You should speak for a just cause and try to get rid of the issue to help everyone.

Even it won't help to solve any problem. Proper communication with trust in the other person is the secret to solving pending problems and they can deal with it themselves without any external assistance.

CHAPTER 3

Personal Self-Defense Against Manipulators

There are two ways of personal self-defense against manipulators, which are physical and psychological self-defense. The creation of personal self-defense against manipulators involves a strong capacity for self-confidence. If you are positive-minded, it loosens a manipulator's control over your thoughts and actions.

Many cults use many strategies to appeal to new adherents and potentially cause you and your family financial and physical harm. Here are some actionable measures to combat those who try to manipulate you.

Tell them you're feeling stressed.

Tell them you feel stressed and don't want to do something. Listen and chat when your subconscious tells you that something is wrong. The quicker you say it, the better as it will not fester and become a more important issue. It is important to know that you have the freedom not to be under pressure to do what you want to do.

Please ask questions.

Ask a variety of questions. The manipulator will consider your questions and this will give you time to reorganize your thoughts and behavior. Consider using any of the following questions as a reference guide:

a.   What am I going to get out of it?

b.   Does what you want from me sound fair?

c.   Can I have a say here?

d.   Do you ask me?

e.   Does that seem to be reasonable?

Reject the submission

When someone comes to you and wants you to do anything, don't do it. At first, this can seem confusing, but at this stage, it will save your lives. Often, the manipulator can be shocked and back down when you say "no."

Don't go on trying to change your mind

If someone sends a message you're not interested in, say no. You are entitled to your actions, thoughts, and emotions and you have no need to give excuses to explain your behavior. You are entitled to change your mind and offer no reason. You have the right to say "no" without feeling guilty.

Face the individual

Analyze the manipulator in a private setting. A public atmosphere can turn followers against you, or worse, alienate you from the mindset of group thinking. Then you will feel obliged and unwilling to meet the requirements.

If you share your feelings, it demonstrates that you are not easily persuaded and that your effort might not be worth it. Also, remember that the individual does not want the relationship to continue. Don't feel guilty again because you have the right to critical thoughts and to judge your actions.

Don't flatter yourself

Flattery is a great manipulative weapon. They use your self- awareness against you. If someone particularly praises you when you have done little to merit it, doubt the purpose. It may be easy to flatter, but it is one of the manipulator's best tools for controlling your thoughts and behavior.

Stop exploitation

Don't give room for someone that makes you feel exploited. Avoiding others doesn't mean you have to end a relationship, it simply means that you try to control the occasions and circumstances.

CHAPTER 4

Manipulate - Do You Unwittingly Do This

Have you ever tried to manipulate anyone? They do what you want so no worries and you may feel good about it. However, there may be signs of frustration from the other person, whether it's your spouse or child at home or co-worker.

One potential explanation for this may be that you try to exploit them in the way you do simply to get them to satisfy your needs. There need to be no wrong intentions, but others will see what we are, based on our actions.

Success in influencing others if this occurs, there are obvious consequences.

The other person may have questions about what to do. You will feel upset if they do not behave according to your wishes or maybe they feel like they have no choice but to follow your lead. The cumulative effect of manipulation, in extreme situations, makes the victim feel helpless.

In the case of Paul and Natalie Hemming, all of these signs were present.

Manipulative behavior in this instance gives a glimpse of what happens if one partner decides to find his way, irrespective of the desire of the other.

Paul kept promising to marry Natalie. Natalie purchased a dress, told her friends, and also made exciting plans. Paul also booked a place

—with her mother's money—yet he called the wedding off three times.

He declined to attend the family reunion when their children were baptized. He said when he got a job at a Mercedes Dealer, "I'll pay you to stay at home." He also refused to allow the eldest daughter of Natalie to see her dad. He had access to her mail for checking her bank statements. The result of all Paul's manipulation and irrational behavior was that he was left by Natalie.

What does manipulate others mean?

In most relationships, both partners may try to influence the other to some extent. This doesn't mean manipulation inherently. To influence the other person, one also uses subtle and manipulative energy.

No act of self-manipulation can be regarded as evil. I would say it is only when you look at the action pattern that you know what is happening.

Some people may realize and try to stop their wish to exploit others.

How we exploit others

If you conduct yourself in one or more of the following ways, you may want to stop exploiting someone:

To falsely request and continuously convey something from the other person is an unreasonable demand. For example, it may be a challenge for a worker to work unpaid overtime.

Threats to put a partner before others

Be judgmental by falsely accusing the other person of being greedy or reckless.

Pulling someone down: this can be very subtle like a stern look or expression, disagreeable voice tone, sarcastic remarks or overt sarcasm.

To mislead the other person by making false statements and saying that insults were just a joke.

You don't want to penalize their actions by screaming, weeping, "silent treatment," making explosive anger or shouting for compliance.

Self-orientation as a manipulation trigger

Most of us try to exploit others in our way, even from time to time, without being obvious. One factor is the idea that we have a normal self-orientation tendency, a trait that can lead to egoism.

Just as you might suggest, how else in this competitive environment can we survive?

However, the normal spiritual approach should take into account people's needs: not prioritizing yourself but sharing yourself with others. Maybe we should ask this question. Is there a danger that self-orientation will be the core of our motives? In other words, do we have a self-concern that goes beyond respecting other people's rights?

It seems that when self-direction rules, we still want to go our way, to win the fight and be seen to be right, to feel superior to others. Does

such an attitude indicate that we want to exploit others so that we have self-interest control?

The bad news is that manipulation can only lead to poor personal ties. This means that we will lose the possibility of a relationship of shared respect and care.

CHAPTER 5

Manipulation in Relationships

Frequently, exploited people appear to be marked and used by manipulators in a variety of different personality types. These are like manipulator trigger buttons. The first step to minimizing manipulation is to know the buttons in your life.

What are the psychological keywords?

1. Its approval and acceptance are very important

Almost everyone wants to be liked and welcomed. That's normal. But many people have much more need of validation than other people, possibly because of their genetic heritage and/or life circumstances. The more you like, the more likely you are to exploit.

A manipulator can hold people in a constant state of fear and a strong need for validation by never complimenting or seeing something positive about what you are doing. Consider yourself working hard during the day only to then get an awkward message regarding a small flaw after a lot of excellent work.

2. Fear of bad emotions

Some people are particularly vulnerable to strong negative feelings, conflict, or confrontation. This means that they change their actions

to prevent frustration or conflict, almost always at a cost to yourself or to someone you serve.

Some manipulators purposely look or start to raise their voices to cause their target to feel upset or stressed. Think of the whipped dog that squeaks when a hand is slightly lifted. It shrinks and reduces itself by changing its actions to reduce the perceived hazard.

3.   Being friendly people and being good

Nothing's wrong with being good. However, there is an issue when you continually ignore your desires for others' sake. How do you know if you're friendly?

Do you burst into an activity to support others because they stated a need, and then lament under your breath how little time you have to do your things?

Can you send it to someone even more than you do? Then you might be friendly people.

There is typically a strong element of "if I am nice to others, then they won't hurt me."

What about Mother Theresa? She gave up a lot for others.

Mother Theresa was not a pleasurable person. People like Mother Theresa support others on their terms and their share of relationships can be managed.

4.   Loss of faith

If you find it hard to say no, you cannot be assertive. Overly assertive people are generally not nice to people. You have two issues because you are both firmly opposed to negative emotions.

Sometimes, a lack of trust is related to vulnerability and a fear of negative answers to your needs or desires. No, you cannot be anxious, nervous or unhappy when you say no. You can still feel exasperated and frustrated at yourself every time you are taken advantage of.5. Poor self-confidence

People who depend on themselves are very unsure of their judgment and skill. They also have very little self-direction. In past generations, many married and highly skilled women had reduced self-sufficiency because they weren't expected to be masters of their destiny, particularly outside the home.

People with low autonomy can generally be seen by the way that they actively seek knowledge about most of their pending and basic decisions. Low self-confidence makes it easy for a manipulator to manipulate and guide you.

You may expect a manipulator to denigrate your knowledge and decisions. Manipulators also lead you quickly to areas of your ability, where THEY can show their vastly superior 'mastery' and add to your feelings of insufficiency.

6.   You know you do not influence your fate

This is similar to low self-dependency but is different because the individual thinks that the outside world governs much more than it does. By comparison, people with a more inward outlook are more assured that they have a great deal of influence over what happens to them.

With an unrealistic world view, you are both open to manipulation and depression.

A major factor in depression is the impression that you manage a continuing negative condition. It's a prescription for depression to be with the manipulator and feeling that you do not influence life. Your manipulations and prejudices will take you down a road of learned impotence.

7.   A sense of underdeveloped personality

Do you feel like you're a little insubstantial and insignificant in comparison with your neighbor? You don't know who you are and what you stand for. Do you live your life for others rather than yourself (including on TV)?

Many people have had a childhood that constantly denigrates their importance. They got constant negative reviews and remarks in their sensitive teens. A history like this can impede the growth of an individual and undermine his sense of identity.

To a manipulator, these individuals are a beautiful amorphous tangle, on which they can make their designs. In general, they make you more obedient to their will and to make your life live through them.

Many of you who read this chapter would no doubt know that you have some buttons, these buttons are typically connected to a lack of self-confidence.

Most people have these features to various extents, rendering them susceptible to exploitation. Being conscious of these features is the beginning of improved manipulation resistance.

The real problem arises when these buttons overpower their personalities. For the victims of manipulators, it is particularly necessary to understand that they can and should improve. You can change yourself much better than a manipulator.

CHAPTER 6

Integrity Vs Manipulation

Before I could write in this chapter, I had to look up "integrity" in the dictionary. I had a feeling that I could trust people with honesty. We have heard people say, "Integrity is fundamental to who I am," or "Without integrity, who are you?" But what does that mean exactly?

"Integrity is the opposite of manipulation." Integrity is far more than faith and loyalty, while integrity has a relationship with it;we can have faith in people of integrity.

Honesty is the attribute of integrity, representing a central SELF in our lives. Honesty is involved-that is, respecting ourselves and who we are, instead of "faking it" or lying dishonestly.

We prefer to trust people with honesty because we see their actions steadily over time and are driven by a variety of values and behaviors. They seem to have determined where their spiritual core is, who they are, who they believe they are supposed to be, and who they want to be.

When we see people acting from that moral core with dignity, we can be assured that they will continue to do so.

The definition of manipulation is also meaningful: manipulation means being different from other people and breaking up to get what we want from others. If we do this, the role of our moral core becomes uncertain. People would not know who we are and who our

SELF is. To accomplish what we want or need, we will be what we need to be without dignity.

What is the cause of integrity loss?

I notice that the environments in which I live cause my desire to exploit or say something required to get what I need. You see, if family members, colleagues or bosses have shown time and again that who I am and what my wants or desires are not relevant, and if they are contradictory, deceptive or utterly harmful, then I might have learned that acting in honesty only opens up my authentic self to attack and damage. So I can mask who I am and try to find out what I need best.

Whew! I feel tired just writing about it. What energy is lost in knowing how circumstances can be exploited? I wish I could tell in my work life that I didn't feel so self-protective! But imagine what it would look like to be in such an unhealthy environment and have such manipulation hardwired into your SELF heart.

In people who have not yet developed an internal SELF-feeling, they may not see it because they are not old enough or because they have grown up in environments that were not comfortable or emotionally stable. I'd "become" whatever the people around me expect if I were one of those people.

I will be "defined" by whoever I was with, the phrase above "amoeba" reflects an organism whose type depends on its container. Maybe "amoeba-like" people aren't purposely deceptive, and we should not think them unethical. However, they cannot act with dignity without a sense of SELF or spiritual centeredness.

Why do we act with integrity?

Well, some of us have divine reasons for integrity. We have decided to obey "GOD" and have embraced the principles that accompany the decision. Some of us have inherited a series of values from our families or cultures and have either deliberately chosen to proceed, unconsciously accepted these values, or are afraid of the consequences of not adopting these practices.

But wouldn't it be better to have a moral compass and always obey it?

It's mentally tiring to guess what everyone around you wants and does. Without understanding ourselves and selecting a moral base, what happens if we see them lead in various directions?

What happens when your kids want something and your wife wants something else?

What if your boss wants something that clashes with your family needs from you?

What happens if stockholders continue to maximize their income to the detriment of the environment or human health?

How can you decide which path to take without a moral base, a set of guiding principles?

How do you find the "compass?"

Sometimes character-forming takes only the decision we can make if we wish to do the right thing. Integrity is a virtue which evolves as we determine what the "right thing" is in different situations.

Integrity, however, includes understanding who we are before we can behave or decide how we want to live.

The suggested steps are therefore possibly more psychological than the steps needed for other virtues.

Only start by asking yourself:

Who am I?

What do I feel, think, need, or want?

What are my strengths and abilities and DO all of them make me happy or satisfy me?

If I had to mention ten features describing my life, what would they be?

How do I live these features consistently? When do I trust myself most?

What do I need to do to change the way I live consistently?

Use the space below to answer these questions and then start to act systematically on what you find out. A journal may be appropriate for continuous self-investigation to establish integrity.

CHAPTER 7

Miscommunication Allows Manipulation

Miscommunication also occurs with people, especially those who do not want to understand what it means. A lot of the problem is innocence because we are all treated differently and have different definitions of what we see as common words. There were so many reasons because of the mixture of confusion and ego. When we get hit, it's a time of war for some of us.

How do we resolve this lack of communication?

Sincerity helps, but it's not enough. Often we have to figure out exactly what we mean and that's where sincerity comes in. First, we have to be frank and admit our true feelings. So we must be frank with others and tell the facts, preferably in a non-violent manner. The only way for us to compromise without manipulation is to speak frankly and value the interests of others and our own.

It does not work to put someone else first and ignore one's feelings and needs because it will stimulate anger and 'little red hen syndrome.' When someone who declined help, tries to do it by himself but in the end, it just doesn't work. The egoistic citizens must note that activity such as this is not tolerated. The astrologers say that Pluto's power brings out the facts, uncovering the slime beneath it all.

Since so many people want to get what they can from others, we have to be very specific about our agreement's parameters. Then we must keep the line when attempting to push and cross the boundaries.

This saying that you give an inch and take a mile refers to these cases. You can typically tell whether someone is trying to exploit previously defined limits. They get upset when they know the borders and need an explanation as to why they cannot.

First and foremost, that's just disrespectful. Secondly, no clarification is owed. For many reasons, some of us give them one anyway. Some people only want others to believe that they are good.

Others just want to stop unintentionally harming the feelings of others, if possible. Most manipulators keep pushing their point and think that they win by humiliating the individual whose limits they cross.

In the face of such an attack and they don't make any mistake, this is certainly a laughing start in front of the manipulator. Notice that they are incredibly blunt and you find it hysterically amusing that they believe an explanation is needed.

Their disrespectful conduct is enough reason to refuse them what they want. Then tell them to quit and take everything, including their bad negative energies, with them.

Most of us were brought up to be honest, compassionate people. We are too sweet for our good and the world's manipulators are more

than happy to show us how weak we are in our treatment. Some of us took a lifetime to learn; some would never learn in this lifetime.

If you are someone who is easily influenced, note this: first take care of yourself. If something else is left after your needs are satisfied, you will determine if you want to support anyone else. You will live a happier life that's less resentful.

Dealing with Emotional Manipulators

You need to know how to deal with emotional manipulators. I agree that there are a few places where it is riper than health care. It is unlikely to be found in natural health care, maybe not impossible, but doubtful because the whole environment is much more comfortable.

You saw it yourself at some point.

Doctors, veterinarians, and their employees just believe they have the solutions to proper healthcare and so they try to find every means to make you guilty. You are far more likely to consider their ways in this way. If you like, you're tested.

Guilt is the biggest reaction when you're emotionally distressed. This can become a question and a source of "what ifs." Guilt and worry are weak feelings that have nothing to do with reality or decent health care.

If you choose not to vaccinate your child or pet, if you have to consult a doctor, a hospital, or a veterinarian on any other for unrelated matters, you are likely to face emotional hazards.

If you have not taken the medicine you claim to have stopped or treated, and a blood test indicates (I intentionally use that word as no test is completely conclusive) that the condition exists, you are potentially subjected to a river of emotional violence, often diluted, but not always watered down. You are likely to be pressurized, even threatened, if you do not want to take traditional cancer care.

Emotional manipulators are operating from an incredibly vulnerable position. If something is fine, no strategies are needed. It is interesting that such techniques still need to be used in traditional medicine, which is so commonly practiced.

Are you scared of anything?

When you have been stirred up by guilt and anxiety, you are in a vulnerable spot. You will never judge soundly.

You can't say the right thing about yourself, your child or your pet. These voices were drowned out. It is almost too late to make an educated decision.

Before it re-emerges, you must learn to cope with emotional manipulation. The first thing to do is to accept this. The guilt and concern were purposely inculcated in you. You'll probably not get rid of it easily, so you have to deal with it.

When you understand that something is happening in you, become mindful of your breathing. Keep it slow and quiet. Don't make it fast. Quick breathing accelerates the pulse and then all is lost.

Listen to the individual politically. Don't let your potential lack of ways bother you. Don't accept, just thank them for their concern and say that you will think about it. Smile slightly if that makes you feel better. Then remove yourself as quickly as possible (and your child or pet).

They may have a legitimate point, but only when you are cool and rational can you see that. Make sure you are cool and rational and look at all options before you take action.

You may want a second opinion or test yourself. You can come from a different way of thinking, maybe a better one. However, one thing is clear, you are not treated with dignity when you feel guilty or concerned about your actions. Perhaps it's time to meet someone who wants to.

It is very rewarding to learn how to deal with emotional manipulators since they place you firmly in the driver's seat. None of us has all or anywhere near the answers. Our memories, emotions, and instincts lead us all the best. Yeah, maybe you make mistakes or feel guilty, but that is because you took extra care to try to make the right decisions, not that you were overruled or exploited.

CHAPTER 8

―――――― ⬳ ――――――

The Basics Of Mind Control

Before you start using proven strategies of mind control, you need to realize that everyone is special, which implies that they have their coping methods. You must then use slight variations of these techniques to fit the tastes and preferences of that individual.

The first step in decrypting is to define the dominant sense of choice and to determine whether to see, hear or sound.

Others will believe you based on what you show- your personality, way of life, and body language. Some people will believe you based on what your friends or colleagues are saying. Others believe in their intuition and use their emotions to direct their decisions.

Can you now see how important this knowledge is?

I will continue to explain how to use the loophole to gain access to the mind of an individual. Before we proceed, promise yourself that you can ethically use these mind control strategies. You will use this to have fun but not to hurt others with your mates.

Bear in mind that by using these strategies, your reputation is on the line. But don't worry, as these methods are discreet, so you can use them without anyone being aware of them. One thing you need to be sure of is who you want to use these mind-control strategies on.

When your target has been identified, track it closely and decode your processing system. If you know what the dominant determining factor (seeing, hearing, or feeling) is, you can adjust circumstances to your objective.

For example, when the person's dominant processing system sees you, take a close look at your behavior. If your hearing tries to find a mutual friend to make them feel like you're a good person to make them talk about you.

This helps the message to hit your target. If your aim of the 'feeling' type is to observe similarly related goals and see which type of person they are and emulate those features, go one step further and inflate attractive features and deflate those the objective hates.

Bear in mind that we talk about mind control and not about 'being the coolest guy or gal in town,' which bragging about yourself might not be an overall attractive function.

Know that you only have one goal-to get space for your dream. Once you've done what you want, you can still change your behavior. If you've done everything right, the goal will always be in touch with you.

After this goal is reached, you now hold the strings and you can move it to the left and right whatever you want, and the individual will satisfy your requests without knowing why.

Here are some established methods of mind control, which you can use to manage your mind and make a happier person. The first thing you have to do is learn how to relax and do some respiratory exercises.

One of the things you need to do is to learn how as a person you can reach your goal and ensure you can relax. One thing about the mind is that it's full of clutter, and the pressure of our jobs and personal lives comes from our daily living.

Breathing exercises are necessary because you try to control yourself and you have seen that if you can do this, you can then dig through the inner reaches of your mind to benefit from it and speak to your subconscious. This is the only way for you to move your mind to another level and better yourself.

The most negative things in the mind surround the subconscious mind, and proven strategies for breathing and relaxation allow us to reprogram the subconscious.

One thing to remember is that yoga and aromatherapy techniques are very good ways to control your mind effectively in an environment where you can speak to the subconscious. The other thing that you can benefit from is the reinforcement method, which helps the mind believe in those messages and think positively, using the New Age theory of optimistic messages.

One thing we do everyday is that we think negatively and what this simply means is that we do not behave as 100% competent individuals. Affirmation is simply the way to write encouraging words on a document and to talk to ourselves every day. When this happens, the subconscious continues to transmit this message every day, and we tend to believe in it.

This technique is very common in some circles, and it helps some religious groups to increase their self-determination and take away the fear of some of their members. While the effectiveness of this technique is disputed, some people and supporters of this approach say it's the best technique there that involves no technology or medicine.

Another way of exploring new technology such as brainwave entertainment, is touse brainwaves to concentrate the mind on areas of change and better improve the strength of the mind. So, here are some of the things you need to get to know about proven strategies for mind control.

CHAPTER 9

How To Recognize Mind Control Techniques

It may sound daunting to learn behavioral health strategies, but it isn't as terrifying or challenging as it sounds. This is a hidden and subtle activity that requires skill, charm, and manipulative strength.

Do you have these features? Don't worry. Mind control strategies are the best place to begin personal growth.

Mind control must not be difficult. Most mind management strategies are quite basic. You will be shocked by how quickly the fundamental basis of this activity is constructed.

You have to ask yourself first:

Why do you want to learn these techniques? What are the objectives?

Why and how do you want to improve the actions of those around you?

You're tired and depressed like most Americans. You want to feel like you've got control again.

According to a new Gallup study, the proportion of satisfied Americans has decreased.

Less than half of Americans feel happier than depressed. Meanwhile, the number of depressed people has gone up.

You can learn mind control strategies and processes if you are included in this disgruntled volume, or even if you find yourself wanting something that you don't have – promotion, love life, income, meaningful relationships. Think of how less frustrating daily life would be if people were to do the things they wanted to.

Fortunately, you do not need a degree in psychotherapy to take controls and procedures into consideration. So what are the fundamentals? Read on:

Wait, watch!

You must understand mind control methods before you can become a master. As you understand people, you get a good idea about where they stand with you. Some gravitate towards you naturally while some do not. You need to know this knowledge before you attempt to have any impact.

Establish faith and confidence

The reasons for this are obvious: the more people trust you, the more likely they are to open up to you and the more open they are, the more receptive it will be to your ideas and suggestions.

Developing relationships not only allows you to develop lasting relationships but also makes people open to the methods of mind control you want to learn.

How can you develop a relationship?

Be a good listener.

Master conversational art. Maintain speed with the person with whom you speak. If it's an engine voice, speed up. Slow down if they're slow and quick. You do the same when you use a lot of hand motions when you talk. This mirroring act lets people know that you "understand" them and that you are part of their world. Be subtle.

Keep calm

People are more vulnerable to behavioral management strategies if they feel like they have given up some control. Don't lose your cool. Don't go to the predetermined response to a tough situation where necessary. Let's say that your sales manager creates a stir over your department's dwindling numbers, maintain a positive attitude despite all the chaos.

It will take people off the ground and make them look inward. Use this self-doubt factor for your benefit. This is the ideal time for you to go through your mind locks with hidden feedback and clandestine manipulation.

Be the force

Take care of the conditions as far as possible. Don't let people benefit from you. When people assume that you are the person responsible, they are more likely to be accessible to you, leaving their subconscious susceptible to your mind management techniques.

Regardless of your situation, these strategies will help you professionally and socially, contributing to a happier and more satisfying life in all fields.

CHAPTER 10

Types of Mind Control Techniques

Mind control methods are also sometimes called brainwashing tactics. These strategies are psychological methods used to influence the emotions, feelings, reactions, behaviors, choices, and ideas of a subject. The person is forced to give control of his mind to someone else through any number of steps. These methods are used for bad purposes more often than for good.

Mind management methods are highly controversial, and science, neuroscientist, psychologist, and sociologist experiments have been extensively discussed and researched. Ethical problems are still included in the discussion.

In certain ways, both extreme and much less severe and seemingly transparent mind control methods are used in, for example, religious sects, military schools, totalitarian states and black operations, terrorism, torture, cell abuse, psychiatric hospitals, parental alienation and individual syndrome.

Subliminal ads and indoctrination provide a milder form of mind control. Mind control was used as a prosecution technique during trial but was dismissed by the court. A variety of other court cases involving New Religious Movements also attempted to justify the use of mind control but was often dismissed.

Brainwashing is carried out in a range of ways. One approach is also paired with other methods to accelerate the procedure. Suggestibility techniques such as hypnosis are used.

These are commonly identified as meditation and relaxation practices. Repeated music is a form of hypnotic mind control where music is performed during 'study sessions.' The music rhythm also has a rhythm closely similar to the heartbeat, i.e. 45 to 72 beats per minute.

Voice roll is another method that lawyers frequently use. This style is peaceful and helps to trigger a trance.

The speaker emphasizes every word in a patterned and monotonous manner, 45 to 60 beats per minute, and can be highly hypnotic. The "feel" space is another hypnotic technique. The room atmosphere, in terms of temperature and light, plays a vital part in the person being hypnotized.

Such widely used methods of mind control include social pressure, denial of older principles, 'heart bombing,' contradictory ideology, privacy loss, and verbal violence.

Other examples are uncompromising rules, clothing codes, financial obligations, religion, regulated acceptance, finger-pointing, sports, dietary adjustments (substance use), and a no question policy.

When you speak about three concepts of the re-education of a person into techniques of mind control, repetition is easily brought into action, accompanied by pedagogical exercises, in which the person is kept busy and not given time to think or focus alone.

Mind control has always been a real means of taking over what is happening in your mind and others. These methods can be easily mastered if you pay the price of learning how to proceed.

Mind control is simply a special skill that you can master. You can gain a lot if you can understand the strategies involved. There are three excellent explanations of why these strategies should be taught. Let's look at them.

1.   Bothering the mind to gain power

You need to learn different methods of mind control to deal with your mind's trouble. The human mind is, in most instances, the location for thoughts and actions. If you can't control what's going on in your mind, life can be boring. You must use these simple strategies to take over your mind and better your life.

2.   To gain the desired attention from others

If you have to win with others in some form of debate, you have to learn these techniques. You can still get the audience to do or say what you want by using powerful mind control strategies while giving a lecture or a speech. You are sure to get all the love you need if you use control strategies to win your heart.

3.   Control of other people's minds

If you take time to gain power, you can easily manage to manipulate the minds of others at will. You must be vigilant of this because your

actions will adversely affect the minds of others. You must concentrate on using the methods that you have learned positively. In this way, you can change other people's lives.

If you have to grasp the above three key explanations, you just need to spend time studying the fundamental principles. You have to spend some time every day practicing the techniques. To succeed in the process, you must use the technique of meditation and visualization.

In most situations, meditation helps a lot in mind control. If you want to see better results, you have to work.

Again, when you practice mind control methods, you have to indulge in the influence of constructive thought and confession. This will allow you to get better outcomes by using the methods to influence the minds of others.

In all, when you take time to explore what you are, you can master these techniques. It is necessary to use any available resource to master the techniques. You will better your life and that of others if you can learn the simple techniques of control that are already proven.

CHAPTER 11

Hypnotic Mind Control Strategies That Put People Under Pressure

Like everything in this world, hypnotic mind control methods come with a certain kind of liability. You can find success, become an inspirational leader or spread more goodness in society. However, if you're not careful, you can also blow your lip.

Scientific Hypnotic Mind Control Techniques 1: Like attracts

It's not hard to get someone to like you, as long as you are observant. When you find someone who likes you, it's far easier for THEM to agree to whatever you suggest. See, the more you like a guy, the more he is inclined to say yes to you.

If you want others to vote, it would be easier to make them want you and do your best. Why do you think politicians are wasting so much time and money on campaigning?

One way to make someone like you is to let them know that you like them first, and then they prefer to like you. Perhaps more important is to let a friend or relative of that person know what you want because it turns out to be more honest and genuine.

2: Use Family Terms

People are reluctant to constantly use the same terms. Some people prefer to use the word "agreed" to end meetings, while others like to use the term "settled."If you are trying to manipulate people's minds, you need to listen to the person you speak those words with and then continue to use the same word.

It creates a fast link or camaraderie between you and the other person, which is important especially if you don't know the other person very well.

3: Nodding Order

If you want someone to tell you "yes," this is a tip that will come handy in the future.

When asked whether they love your idea or not, ask, "Good, isn't it?" and then nod your head. The nod leads them to say "yes,"whether or not they have made up their minds.

At first, nodding may seem very strange but others may not notice it until you point it out. Using this nodding technique and with little effort, you will have some positive reactions.

When used for success, hypnotic behavioral stimulation methods can have such a beautiful and optimistic influence on society. Make sure that what you are doing would not harm others until using these mind-control tricks to manipulate people. Use them carefully and with some responsibility.

NLP Mind Control Techniques

I guess you might be interested in NLP mind management strategies, but don't know where to start. Don't worry. I will give you a quick summary of NLP and I will share some of the favorite techniques with you as we proceed.

First and foremost, NLP stands for Neuro-Linguistic Programming. You can already deduce from the word itself that NLP has something to do with interacting with the mind of an individual.

One of the most important concepts of NLP is the interconnectedness of mind and body. The way you move (or don't move) shows what you think and feel. Similarly, how your body moves impacts your thinking.

If you want to change your mindset, start with your physiology. For example, if you want to exude confidence, why don't you sit taller and straighter? Smile at the people around you confidently, even though you don't necessarily feel courageous. These little changes will turn into your subconscious, and you will soon feel positive for real.

2: Emphasize key terms

It can be very important to emphasize key terms in a conversation. For example, if you want to persuade a person to attend an event, emphasize your orders.

Say, "Meet up at the W Hotel." Then, "Friday night. 7:30." This is more likely to get a positive response. Note that you don't even have to ask people if they want to come. You may automatically define the invitation as a confirmation.

3: Power Visualization

If you already see yourself doing what you want, you will be able to pursue that path without difficulty. Visualization is so important that many people resort to it to fulfill their aspirations and dreams. For example, people who want to lose weight depend on visualization to stay healthy and happy. They already picture their ideal weight and keep the lifestyle up.

As you have discovered, NLP mind control strategies are not only useful in self-development, they also enable people to follow your lead. Use this information wisely and spread the word freely.

Mind Control Techniques Through Brainwave Entrainment

Mind control governs your life ultimately, and while we all want to have this power at our side, the fact is that we are not born of the ability to go into the depth of our mind and put into our hands. The irony of this problem is that we do not have a mental power to control our mind. We are simply confined to ourselves and that may be the toughest competition ever to succeed in improving ourselves and personal development.

For this reason, many people struggle, plans for the New Year go down the drains and we continue to be the same dysfunctional person as everybody knows. We're up against each other, and we win most of the time. That means that we lose at the same time and the only way to do so is to isolate ourselves from ourselves, and as contradictory as this may seem, it is to place us in a state in which the unconscious is divided from the conscious mind: dividing the dualities of mind.

If we can do this, the playground is fair, and we can reprogram "ourselves" or our subconscious mind, the other, to avoid blocking our path to success. This explanation would be identical to the whole theory of Dr. Jekyll and Mr. Hyde.

If we can distinguish the conscious and the subconscious, we can get rid of all the bad habits, bad orders, and bad patterns of behavior which have been within the subconscious-the very ones which rule our lives.

How can you do this?

Yeah, there are some different forms. Whether you are a Swami or Kung-Fu master, you can train your mind to break yourself into a deep meditation that has the same impact as self-hypnosis. If you are in this place, you can cleanse yourself from the bad things. Unfortunately, we can't yet do so, and science has broken through and filled the void, which helps us to do the very same thing. These innovations include the application of affirmations or constructive

feedback bombardment, binaural beats autosuggestion, and subliminal messages. The most common type of this mind-control technology is brainwave entertainment, and it uses forms and series of sounds and visual stimuli to activate the brain in certain frequency conditions. It is a state that lulls the brain into meditation and permits one to explicitly instruct the subconscious mind with messages and enticing stimulants.

This means that we can do something, start bad habits like smoking, and can inspire each other to work harder, be more optimistic, be positive, or wipe out public fear. There are hundreds of applications and you'll find one that's right for you.

CHAPTER 12

Mind Control Techniques To Live In Happiness And Get What You Want

Many people are shocked that they have a lot of money, power, and place, but they lack freshness in physical and mental life. It affects your business, so you are worried and unhappy.

They don't have faith in spirituality, but they want to buy a mind- control technique to live spiritually content. They want to run their major businesses and cannot waste time reading eBooks or attending sessions of spirituality.

All of those people are coming to me. The recurring question is, "How can you buy happiness and a mind-control strategy that is free to attend any classes of spirituality and /or read holy writings and eBook of masters of spirituality?

The general character of people is to live life in the subconscious mind lost in four big misunderstandings. They make mistaken thoughts about some subjects as permanent, which are only transitory;

they also make mistaken thoughts about some objects and subjects as a source of purity, which in reality creates an impurity in the mind.

If you practice the art to better understand and control your senses and how they affect your thoughts in the simple mind, most of the signs of unhappiness are lost even in the worst physical living conditions.

This mental rule induces unhappiness in most people, mistaking temporary subjects as permanent in thoughts, unclean subjects as pure in thoughts, the giving of pain as a giver of pleasure, and the false personality as a genuine self.

Everybody in the world, including the physical mind and body perceptions that are evolving rapidly, have no link to a real self in consciousness. In sub-consciousness, any wrong interaction with the physical world is always irritating. Deep meditation helps you feel and see this reality.

Consider your physical body as an instrument of mind control and control over all of its actions. To keep your physical body comfortable, a good diet and sleep are more important. It is more appropriate to regulate impurity in thoughts and egoism through daily meditation, to keep your mind happy.

It is a fallacy to assume that the greater the income, power and status of the people means the more happiness. However, these reduce the percentage of quietness and satisfaction in mind. A recent study reveals that the average individual in the United States lives in more happiness than the wealthier.

One day, in meditation, I sat before the sculpture of my physical body from birth to death and realized that my physical body was very ephemeral and fake. My mind control was set to hear the internal sounds of a pleasant subtle existence. I heard many of my likes and dislikes in many things, which are temporary and evolving everyday.

A friend who had come to learn mind control methods and to live in spiritual gladness feared to see me dead in the physical body of sculpture. I advised him to do similar therapy at home everyday, and I guarantee him refreshment and peace in his life. It may be difficult to do this meditation for many initial days.

Mind control strategies are very useful because they generally provide people with major benefits in their lives, particularly in their businesses and careers. The way others think and respond is a good way to win debates and prevent more confrontations.

However, these methods should not be used to exert pressure on other people to do what they want. They're good for your job.

The only way to achieve this is to use legal methods of mental health.

One effective strategy of mental discipline is the use of the Favor Bank Method. This system helps others to feel grateful to you without a great deal of intimidation. This is just the way you have used the favors that you have offered others in the past. They clearly owe you, so you just subtly ask them to return the favor. It's like relying on the people you helped.

Another strategy is sitting at the Winners' Table.

You can make them believe you're always right when you hang out with the winners. Try to align yourself as much as possible with those who support the company and society in general.

In doing so, others will see you as trustworthy and highly honest, making them more likely to believe in your cause. If you stay close to powerful people, you will have the ability to influence others, which allows you to accomplish what you want.

One of the trickiest methods for mental discipline is to keep the cards hidden. It only makes sure you don't show your cards to anyone so you won't risk your asses. You don't have to be a card player and it's not a risky game.

It is a very subtle way to ensure that you have complete control over anything that happens in your life. Your secret cards act as a contingency plan if your original objectives fail. A good example is offering discounts on street markets.

If you seem rich and arrogant, any trader will look at you as someone who can buy something at a control price, so why give you a

discount? You dress like a millionaire and leave your cards open. If you dress up beautifully, you cover your asses. Even if you can afford a product's normal price, you still have reasonable chances of a good price drop. The power of persuasion is one of the simplest methods of mind control. You may have used this strategy when you were a kid if you think about it. This is just so people can see how you do without being too pushy. If you ask someone persuasively for something, he will feel ashamed to reject your offer.

The use of intellectual management methods is just a way to ask for more. However, it should not go beyond reasonable limits. If you take advantage of these strategies when the other person loses too much, it would not be the ethical approach.

CHAPTER 13

What Is Emotional Intelligence?

When you recognize emotional intelligence, you can see those around you and those who don't: at work, in politics, in the media, and around you. The media use both EI and EQ as emotional intelligence shortcuts.

Emotional intelligence reflects empathy. It is the ability to "read" the feelings of other people and to respond adequately. Emotionally smart people excel because they have strong relationships with others, confidence and love.

They trust you and learn to trust you when you understand how and when you are compassionate, encouraging, honest, trustworthy or caring towards people. This provides a structure to create a sustainable, positive relationship between companies and people.

To cultivate emotional intelligence, you must learn not only to concentrate on your own needs and desires but also on others' needs and wants. This calls for slow gratification, persistence and commitment to more than the bottom line.

Emotional intelligence is often basically emotional awareness, indicating that your mind can control your emotions.

According to Goleman, emotional intelligence has five characteristics: self- awareness, self-control, motivation, empathy, and social skills.

•   Self-consciousness: people with high IT realize their emotions, but they don't let their thoughts control them. You know the difference between the emotions and the thoughts and can use reasoning without denying or quashing them to control emotions.

They are optimistic because they have faith in their instincts and good judgment, which is a product of using emotions and critical reasoning to evaluate situations. People with emotional intelligence can take a rational look at themselves.

They know their strengths and weaknesses and work in these fields to improve their results. They are genuinely optimistic about themselves, which means that they have fair expectations of good behavior.

They care for others but they are not dependent on one another. They should set limits for self-protection. This knowledge of oneself is an important basis for EI.

•   Self-control: This is often referred to as self-control and impulse control, meaning that feelings and desires can be regulated. Individuals who self-regulate normally do not allow themselves to become overly angry or jealous; they are not agitated or emotional and do not make impulsive and insensitive choices.

You think before behaving or responding. Self-control attributes are thoughtfulness, security, honesty, and the willingness to say no. They are excellent at delayed fulfillment, recognizing that they could

achieve better results by waiting for what they want. They work on an internal ethics code, not an externally imposed norm of conduct.

•   Motivation: usually people with a high level of EI are inspired. They can delay immediate results for long-term success. They are very creative, they love a challenge and they are very successful with everything they do. They know that inspiration comes from celebration and gratitude and are ready to inspire yourself and others if possible.

•   Empathy: this is the capacity to recognize and consider your desires, expectations and perspectives. Empathic people know other people's emotions well, even though they may not be apparent.

As a result, empathic people typically handle relationships, listen to and communicate with other people excellently. They stop stereotyping and judging too fast, and live their lives in a transparent, truthful manner. They show compassion and kindness and a good attitude towards others.

•   Social skills: another indicator of high IE is good social skills. You know how to work together, to be team players. Instead of concentrating first on their achievements, they know how success comes by helping others to grow and shine.

They can handle conflicts, are outstanding communicators and experts of relationship building and sustaining. In addition to their empathy, those with high IE often have strong tolerance, kindness, faith, appreciation, compassion, and emotional responsiveness.

This is how you and others understand emotional intelligence:

1.   What is an indication that a person has no EQ at all?

He or she has no idea what to say or think about emotions. "How do you feel about ..." elicits just what, if anything, he or she feels.

2.   What is the downside of someone with little to no emotional understanding?

It's not very rewarding, but we all like emotional intelligence and empathy. It also means that the individual won't listen or sympathize with your experience.

3.   Should we separate ourselves from the individual if we cannot detect any emotional intellect?

If the relationship goes well, it's cool. This question is not going to matter. You may try to explain it, draw it out of your mate, relative, or partner if you are irritated by a lack of emotional intelligence and everything else is good, but it will take a lot of patience. It's like describing a three-year-old's emotion.

4.   What if the person has an EQ? What can you do to help them in creating further EQs?

If your EQ is on view, be very open and welcoming. When he or she is out, be sure to show your gratitude. When she or he listens to you or anyone else sympathetically, compliment him or her.

5.   How do we help others to stay emotionally present and smart?

Be sensitive to him or her emotionally. Offer him or her room to react to you with emotion and thought, do not be impatient.

6.   Why is a strong EQ desirable?

High emotional intelligence generates closeness, support, empathy, and love in your relationship. Having fun or sharing feelings with someone with a high EQ is easy. You can rely on a high-quality person to be kind and patient.

Before starting a new meeting or procedure, kindly take the following steps:

1.   Please remember the mental possibilities:

Will you learn something?

Are you ready to meet a new friend?

Would people just get out of the house and feel good for new things?

2.   Remember your goals: you go there to have fun and enjoy the people.

3.   Check out your good personal qualities:

Why do you want to see your friends? What do they like about you?

Is it your intellect, sense of humor, personality, or ability to talk? Are you a loving and compassionate person?

Remembering these values ensures that you can radiate this good energy.

4.   Have a positive outlook: research suggests that people with a positive outlook live happier lives, partially because an appealing and charming positive attitude attracts people. In turn, you make

friends. If you are optimistic, you help yourself and others, you see more good things than bad things which make connecting to others easier.

5.   Wear stylish but fascinating clothing that represents who you are.

For example, if you like traveling, wear a shirt, scarf, tie or gem of a foreign country, or wear something which reflects your ethnic background, or a hobby (sports, outdoor activities, a surfboard-type Hawaiian shirt, a garden or animal printing). It will help to launch talks.

Combine the energy with the energy of the people around you. The energy level is pretty high if you dance or eat a poolside barbecue. If you have a quiet talk at a cocktail party, discuss books, take a class or sit down for dinner, then the energy is milder and more concentrated.

6.   Be careful: look around you and try to make friends. Note who is around you and what is fascinating or appealing about them, find an odd thing about what you wear and add to it. "Excuse me, I couldn't help but note this beautiful color; it looks amazing at you." or "What's a nice watch?"

7.   Get ready in advance: read interesting forums to learn about a hit film's history, modern technology advancement, or cool new trends. Then you'll have plenty to say when someone wants to talk to you.

8.   Find a way to help:

What do you need to do? I suggest seeking a "job" in a new setting. Don't just say "what can I do to help?" Rather, volunteer for something specific:

Invite people and show them around or refill the food table. It gives you a sense of belonging, a major reason to meet everyone, and you should be busy enough to keep your nervousness away. The hostess will be grateful and will remember you later.

9.   Follow-through: if you meet someone you want to know more, join the event or meet with a coffee invitation. In these social settings, the best friendships start.

CHAPTER 14

Being Emotionally Intelligent

As one with the spirit, our natural existence is a harmonious state of nature, in which the only emotions are constant harmony and happiness. Therefore, if we encounter anything other than peace and happiness, we've got ourselves out of control.

This is because of our conditional and flawed thought, which appears as tolerances, desires, and restricted beliefs. Using our Emotional Intelligence, we can understand the message that the soul sends us through these emotions so that we can correct our thought and thus always step towards love.

Emotionally intelligent is my capacity to perceive my emotional states of being conscious. Being 'emotional' means I am aware of my emotional state of being. Being 'intelligent' means that I know the situation, events, and situations that I currently experience rationally or logically.

I'm intelligent because I can rationalize my truth consciously. I'm emotional if I can sense my energy perception-my emotional energy.

Emotional intelligence loses focus when I confuse emotional with irrational beings.

I learn about my irrational actions without emotional intelligence when I research the negative state of being that causes me to subconsciously respond. I'm looking at 'irrational thinking.'

Emotionalism does not respond irrationally; it knows my emotional state of being conscious. I never respond emotionally because I can still respond intelligently with emotional intelligence. To understand irrational behavior requires emotional awareness, although it is not the concept of emotional intelligence.

Being In A Mental State

Before I understand being intelligent, an emotional 'state of being' requires explanation. If I describe an emotional state of being, it becomes a definite emotion and I know of it consciously.

It is my understanding of the definite essence of my feelings that helps me to be intelligent emotionally.

An 'emotional' person is conscious of his feelings.

An 'Emotionally Intelligent' person can consciously name (define) his emotional state and create it at will. By intelligently identifying an emotion, I also become emotionally aware of the sensation and I become rationally aware of its meaning.

I can't get a certain emotion unless I can describe it. If an emotion is not called, it will remain either a positive or a negative experience, depending upon the convictions I hold in my subconscious.

I describe an emotion (emotional state of being) with a descriptive adjective. Any adjective that defines my emotions or emotional state

is an emotion. An emotion is just a feeling that I don't understand, without an adjective.

My emotional energy reserve

All energy firms have power, magnitude, and potential. Feelings are no different. The power of any energy is understood when the energy's intensity and magnitude come together.

Electric power has a force called 'volts,' an amplitude known as 'amps' and the potential known as 'watts.' All are named after the person who identified them for the first time. Emotional energy is more complicated since its potential is not only divided by force and magnitude but also divided by polarity and magnitude by sex.

The polarity of my feelings is positive or negative, and the nature of my energy is men or women. (Old age and pride are male while modesty and meekness are female. However, impatience and intolerance are generally

considered negative and patience and tolerance positive).

The extent to which my emotional energy is unbalanced, separated by polarity, gender or by both, decides the strength of the emotion I feel. The greater the disparity, the higher the emotional pressure.

The strength of my emotional state is both the product of sex and the polarity of emotional energy.

Emotional intelligence not only includes the concept of my emotional state but also an awareness of its relevance to my life.

Understanding my emotional energy capacity allows me to be mindful of:

o   Its power and scale

o   Its sex, intensity, and polarity

o   The meaning of an adjective

o   The thinking or feelings that support the emotion.

The true power of my emotional energy is the pure feeling of love from my soul.

Life is an expression of emotion

My Emotional Intelligence demands more than my ability to control my unreasonable behavior. It needs the ability to intelligently consider my emotional experiences. The explanation for my unreasonable behavior is my lack of emotional intelligence. I respond irrationally with what is called an emotional response often confusingly.

When I get intelligence and understanding, I reply with positive emotion. My irrational behavior manifestations are triggered by my lack of logical intellect.

Extreme irrational behavior due to a lack of cognitive capacity may be identified by a rational person without emotional comprehension as a mental disorder.

Diagnosing emotional illness or disease does not require logical thinking, so it may be typically diagnosed as physical or mental rather than emotional. In the absence of feelings, my life as a rationally intelligent man became an unemotional existence.

The rationally smarter I get in a dualistic world, the more constrained, unconnected, and emotionally unintelligent I am. My experience is that the more compassionate and optimistic I rationalize my environment, the less I react with the irritation of my rage and intolerance.

However, I prefer to be 'reasonable' with emotional intelligence, rather than compassionate and 'allowing.'. I don't want to be a compassionate patient who tolerates life peacefully any longer. I embrace life now as an emotional experience because I grow to be emotionally mature enough to let it be.

Emotional Intelligence True Test

The true test of my emotional intelligence is whether I am happy and satisfied because of my deliberate decision. My real nature is just the emotional indifference that keeps me from happiness and well-being.

Happiness is a state of emotion. How can a reasonable person be content in an unconnected and unemotional state? Wellness is a mental experience.

How would I feel in a culture that does not take one iota of emotional intelligence for physical and mental illness?

Compassion for others means nothing unless I have described the compassion I feel. Defining compassion as: "Wanting to alleviate the suffering of others" is not the definition of an emotional desire but a rationally logical description of the actual want.

I am separated from my true emotional essence by my lack of emotional intelligence. A rational world has become an irrational

world without real happiness and well-being and full of lies and disease. We have lost our relationship to our true wealth and our true health because, as a society, our emotional intelligence is disconnected.

In an emotionally intelligent culture, one's own emotional experiences question the only irrational behavior. The task for a modern society is to make men emotionally reasonable and to make women reasonable and to realize that there's no difference between the two. The battle of the sexes is then declared over.

CHAPTER 15

Understanding the Significance of Emotional Intelligence

Be wise, follow the footsteps of intelligent people, study, and prepare so that you can also get the expertise they receive. These are the stereotypical comments made by our parents, friends, elderly people, and even the bureau manager.

It means being conscious and knowledgeable in controlling the situation is the secret to discarding the performance formula. What type of information do these guys worry about?

They speak of rational intelligence that involves reasoning, pattern recognition, scientific analysis, innovative and creative ideas decoding, etc. Nearly 90 percent of the population has rational intellect and familiarity with the elderly and community. Therefore, it is clear that logical intelligence will to a certain degree drive your graph of progress but saturates after a point. Knowledge is the panacea for all of your anxiety and suffering. My response is yes, knowledge with feelings and emotions: it is known as emotional intelligence.

Emotional intelligence is the capacity to become conscious of emotions, produce and access emotions,

and control our emotional resources to facilitate our personal and professional development.

The benefit is that if you are fully aware of your emotions and control your actions and responses, you will inspire everyone around you and develop strong relationships and social skills with others and express sympathy for others.

The discovery of IQ (intelligence quotient) was founded in the 20thcentury and people's character was measured based on an intellectual quotient. In layman terms, it is the ability to spin money and make a wealthy individual.

Different inquiries have shown that this is a futile practice. Emotional intelligence is needed to lead a happy, stable and efficient life. Although the smart quotient is measured under certain criteria of chronological and mental age, emotional intelligence does not have any such criteria and can be developed at any point in life.

What are the advantages of EI?

It is a false hypothesis that emotional intelligence is only important in the social arena such as long-term good relations with others but has a significant role to play in every area of life.

The main advantages of emotional intelligence are:

1. Ability to cope favorably with loss and criticism – Less praise and more disappointment in life. An individual with EI knows the strengths and disciplines. He takes

disappointment and evaluation just one step closer to success.

Emotionally intelligent people can understand their emotional condition and other people's emotional conditions and thus interact more effectively with people. Therefore, they connect easier, develop closer ties, gain more success at work and lead a happier life.

John Gottman was right when he said, "In the last decade or so, science has discovered a huge amount of the role that emotions play in our lives."

Emotional intelligence has five essential elements: self-awareness, self-control, inspiration, empathy and social skills. The first three skills are intrapersonal and apply to your experience and management.

Empathy and social skills are interpersonal skills which concern your ability to communicate and work with others. The better your intrapersonal performance, the easier your interpersonal skills are to communicate. Mastering these skills will allow you to live a healthier, happier, stronger and fulfilled life.

The primary component of emotional intelligence is self-awareness. It's the ability to know what feelings you have and why you do. It is easier for you to identify and control your emotions if you accept your emotions and keep your feelings from ruling over you. You are much more positive, so you don't let your feelings get out of hand. Being self-aware also helps you to evaluate yourself, to appreciate your strengths and weaknesses better and to focus on these areas to produce positive results for yourself and others. Self-control is the ability to control your feelings and desires and choose the feelings you like rather than becoming the object of certain emotions. It is easier for you to think before acting if you can control your emotional state, and this prevents you from making impulsive and rash decisions. This ability also helps you to create a more constructive and efficient negative emotion.

Motivation is the third aspect of emotional intelligence. This means that you use your feelings to be hopeful, optimistic and consistent rather than negative and depressive. You seem to be very driven, creative and successful with everything you do if you have a high level of emotional intelligence. You use your feelings wisely and take the right steps to succeed in the face of significant hardship or challenge and to achieve your objectives. Empathy is emotional intelligence's fourth feature. It's the ability to consider and appreciate other people's thoughts and viewpoints. Empathic people generally can listen efficiently and correctly and are usually excellent in the management of interactions, communication changes, establish trust and relationships with others. Social skills are the fifth aspect of emotional intelligence. Emotionally intelligent people possess good social skills and outstanding relationships. If you are highly intelligent emotionally, you do not rely first on your achievements and you still think in the best interests of others. You always cultivate an environment in which people collaborate rather than fight and help others develop and grow. Today, emotional intelligence is a key to success in life and the good news is that whatever your real emotional intelligence level is, you can boost it. It allows you to understand and control your feelings as well as those of others more effectively and lead a happier, healthier and fulfilled life.

CHAPTER 16

How To Develop Your Emotional Intelligence (EI)

The word emotional intelligence, shortened as EI, has much to do with the skill, capacity and ability to discern and measure one's emotions.

Contrasting ideas as to how to identify and use emotional intelligence in the various fields of interest remain in the foreground.

However, irrespective of the different definitions and uses of the notion of emotional intelligence on some subjects which are regarded purely as technical, the term etymology can still be drawn from one of Charles Darwin's works, particularly regarding the importance of emotional expression to survival or subsistence and second adaptation.

While traditional denotations of the word intelligence stressed the cognitive domains during the 1900s, some prominent scholars in the study of intelligence began to recognize the value of non-cognitive domains.

As an example, the word social intelligence, describing other people's ability to understand and handle, was already used in 1920. The word 'emotional intelligence' was first used to refer to Wayne Payne's doctoral thesis, An Analysis of Emotion: Cultivating

Emotional Intelligence. But the word emotional intelligence had appeared in Leuner before this piece of research.

EI and work results have a strong association in some studies. Cote and Miners gave a compensatory hypothesis between IQ und EI that the connection between emotional intelligence and work success is very positive as cognitive intelligence decreases.

Petrides (et. al.) first discussed this concept in 2004 in the sense of academic success. The results of the previous research indicated that workers with low intelligence quotient have better task performance and a citizenship attitude towards the company per se, the higher their emotional intelligence.

In defining the concept of emotional intelligence, let us deal with how the emotional intelligence of a person can be improved. It is surprisingly evident that people with high IE have greater and better opportunities to achieve success in all facets of life.

Before you start taking an emotional intelligence test, remember some concepts that tend to develop an individual's IT. After reading this chapter, all the ideas included in it are supposed to be integrated as their own into the readers.

1)   Deference

This term is not simply a collection of linguistic sound symbols and conveys a meaning. It is more than how dictionaries and encyclopedias describe it. It is not something that can be gained by dramatic means but can be done over time. This remains a hollow idea until people manifest it to others.

Respect is a firm base for the growth of the EI. If you want someone to respect you, you must first learn how to value your feelings or emotions. Mutual deference is then created. The golden rule stresses, "do unto others what you want others to do unto you."

If your office partner is in great difficulty, irrespective of any problem, you should show empathy and compassion and try to find realistic solutions that can minimize his or her issue. If your friend has a different religion, don't pursue a religious discussion that might hurt him or her.

2)   Using reverse psychology techniques

Occasionally it inevitably goes rough or harsh and luck isn't on your side. Just rest if you're upset and not in a good mood; try to be calm in a tough or troubling situation. Though it is easier said than done, always strive to put a true smile on your face. Never fear.

Bear in mind that having issues is like sitting in a rocking chair.It does not take you anywhere and worrying would certainly not add one day to your life, but just the other way round. So why stress yourself if the situation just gets worse.?

3)   Listening

Wars in history could have been prevented if only all the nations representatives had learned to consider one another's views and then attempted to draw up strategies for eradicating those disagreements.

Learn to listen. The most popular people are not loquacious individuals but are the types of people who like to listen to the great ideas of other people and learn from them.

Listening is one of the factors that lead to their enduring success. It can be said that if you are actively listening and learning how to apply the positive ideas you have learned or read, you will excel greatly in all that you do.

The measures to develop your emotional intelligence described earlier can be easily understood, but the first step in improving your IT is to create an understanding of these ideas. The hardest thing is to live it, which depends entirely on you.

CHAPTER 17

Why Emotional Intelligence Is So Vital in This Climate to Ensure Success?

The main premise of emotional intelligence is that EQ skills are linked to how people work effectively with others, especially around:

- Self-consciousness

- Vehicle operations.

- Common consciousness

- Relationships Management

1) Self-consciousness

Self-consciousness requires a good understanding of emotions, strengths, weaknesses, drives and abilities. On the surface of this idea, there is nothing new – it has been celebrated for thousands of years but it's a vital talent and many people lack it.

It is so important that people with high levels of self-awareness know how their emotions and beliefs affect them and how they communicate with each other. You seem to be reflective and you take time to think about things that are important to you and how

your jobs and lives contribute to those topics. This self-reflection allows them to realize and stand up to both their shortcomings and strengths.

2)   Vehicle operations

Goleman says self-administration frees us from being prisoners of our feelings. We can't control our feelings without knowing what we feel and this leaves us at the mercy of our emotions. This is all right in terms of good feelings such as excitement or performance, but it's a problem when we're dominated by bad emotions such as anger or anxiety.

People with this mastery are typically confident, up-to-date, and excited. This is especially important at work, as emotions are infectious.

3)   Social consciousness

The third aspect of Goleman's EQ, Social Knowledge, mainly concerns empathy. It is the ability to interpret the facial expressions, voices, and nonverbal signs of another person to comprehend their emotions.

This is particularly important for leaders because they can say and do what is most suitable by being attuned to how people feel. They can, for example, try to ease people's concerns, lessen rage, or have a nice time at the office party in a more positive example.

4)   Relationships Management

Relationship management requires the integration of all three skills. This is a person's most noticeable aspect, especially leaders. You

see capabilities such as conflict management, team building, and influencing others.

Leaders with strong skills are typically successful in handling relationships in three areas of EQ because they are adapted to their feelings and that means that relationships are approached from a genuine point of view. It's not just nice, but it's what Goleman calls 'friendliness with a goal': pushing people in the way they want to.

These people build networks very well, not just because they are incredibly social, but because they know that nothing is achieved alone and they are willing to collaborate with others. These EQ skills are special in the technological and cognitive skills of an individual.

According to Goleman, 90% of the disparity in success between stars and average performers is due to EQ skills. This and other studies show that EQ skills are more specifically related than conventional acts like IQ to essential business measures and individual achievement. It's not that IQ and common factors don't matter, they are clear but IQ and other c-specific skills, in particular in leadership and management roles, are entry criteria.

One problem that sometimes occurs is whether people are born with high EQ or whether they can be taught. We all know people who are extremely able to collaborate with others. They understand intuitively how to make people happy and, if they are leaders, how to inspire their people and keep them involved.

Sure, some people are simply more talented than others but the good news is that EQ skills can be taught. Clear research has been done on this and strong evidence has been provided that people can learn how to function more efficiently.

Yet people must be personally inspired to do this and they need to practice what they learn on the job and develop their new skills.

Many of us can think of people who are instinctively capable of working together with others. So while EQ is an essential skill, can it be something created, or is it something with which a person is born?

There is research available that clearly shows that EQ can be taught. Dr. Fabio Sala of The Hay Party considers workshop operations to boost EQ effectively. Research at the University of Case Western found that EQ preparation not only increases efficiency but also preserves those benefits over some years.

The good news for businesses is that while genetic predisposition to Emotional Intelligence can occur, those skillscan be developed and sustained for the long term. Training and development are required to develop these skills. Finally, without a real intention, the EQ skills would not be developed.

CHAPTER 18

Is Emotional Intelligence Learning Possible?

While EQ is necessary for almost every work situation, it is of particular importance to the HR group to use EQ to improve their leadership and management efficiency. And everybody has sought to gain more efficiency with less capital in the current demanding environment. This drive for high performance prompted Sales Training International Ltd to analyze EQ more closely.

They actively support organizations through training and development of interpersonal skills. Our experience with companies of all sizes shows that efficient leaders can boost their organizations' efficiency. Certainly, different circumstances involve different methods of leadership.

In practice, a leader with strong EQ skills may evaluate a situation and find a suitable response. Without EQ, a person with high quality, good experience, and good ideas won't be a great leader.

The higher a leader grows, the greater the emotional intelligence is. However, the risk of EQ issues also increases with more senior managers.

Research by Fabio Sala indicated that the disparity in ratings can be attributed to the fact that senior managers usually have fewer feedback opportunities because of their rank, and therefore less likely to provide positive feedback to people in lower positions.

Leadership and EQ

One criticism we sometimes hear of emotional intelligence is that it sounds fantastic in theory, but it is hard to put into practice. And some EQ advocates appear not to be doing a very good job of looking at how it works at the day-to-day job or how it can be applied and changed.

One of the main problems here is that Emotional Intelligence appears to be common. It implies that all people will demonstrate these abilities in more or less the same way. Goleman and his colleagues are adamant that not all successful leaders possess all EQ skills and much of the importance of EQ is situational — certain circumstances are more likely to need some EQ skills than others.

However, what is often ignored is that there is a particular element of conduct that affects how people work and how they perceive the actions of others.

EQ and polyvalence

Organizations in today's economy are searching for ways to increase efficiency. Emotional intelligence has emerged as a platform for enhancing individual and organizational efficiency and as research continues to log, EQ shifts.

EQ's tangible, measurable advantages include improved revenue, stronger recruitment, and retention, and more successful leadership. Besides, proof exists that EQ skills can be built through training

programs. Polyvalence preparation provides unique strategies to improve interpersonal awareness. Developing this skill makes it more effective and profitable for individuals and their organizations.

And last but not least:

1.   The U.S. Air Force has improved its ability to forecast effective recruitment by a triple and decreased recruitment cost by $3 million.

2.   An analysis of over 500 executive search applicants described interpersonal abilities as considerably better markers of performance than intelligence or previous experience.

In all countries and cultures, results were clear.

In both of these cases, emotional intelligence was the predictor. The interest in Emotional Intelligence has increased in recent years, as research has shown its influence on a variety of business behavior. These include recruitment and work selection, sales, relationships and management results.

CHAPTER 19

Amplify Your Strengths with Emotional Intelligence

Juggling your job and your personal lives with conflicting interests leave no time for a change. Where do you concentrate on making the most progress in your time?

There are two basic contributors to your ability to fulfill your capacity beyond the speed you learn (your IQ). The first contribution is to know who you are (your personality), including your strengths.

The second factor is the ability in managing the challenges of life individually and socially. This capacity is emotional awareness or EQ, and it allows you to take advantage of who you are and what you have experienced.

Emotional Attributes and Intelligence:

Positive psychology was the basic concept of the strength movement. Instead of dwelling on your weaknesses, the purpose of the movement is to discover (and develop) what your natural forces are (and have been from a young age).

The main idea is, if you affirm what you are already doing, you can get much quicker. Many things that you are bad at will never be the places where you shine.

Rather than waste your time and resources in mediocrity, you spend it converting your most valuable talents into grandeur.

Specifically, the realization that the brain is hard-wired to handle events emotionally before it can analyze things rationally was the basic concept of emotional intelligence. The goal is to increase your emotional sensitivity so that you can appreciate them and manipulate them to your advantage.

When you develop self-consciousness, you can stop spending your time trying to drive your emotions away and allow them to dominate you. You should now grasp it and use it to your advantage and the advantage of the people around you.

You get much better as you learn to read and manipulate feelings constructively. The great thing about emotional intelligence is that it can be modified. The areas of the brain where emotional intelligence functions are extremely dynamic, as you learn new behaviors the brain adjusts physically, making those behaviors easier for potential use.

How your abilities are affected by emotional intelligence:

Each person, regardless of his occupation or his stage in life, should together develop their strengths and emotional intelligence to make the most of their life's possibilities. You may discover for example that your strengths include ambition, strategic and futureorienteers; but if you don't have self-consciousness and self- management, it is difficult to turn these strengths into personal or professional success.

Imagine a genuine visionary with the desire to succeed and the willingness to see how to get there. If they are obligated to win every interaction with someone they meet, they may not know that it is just the worst time to press too hard and risk the help of the main allies they need to get their vision off the ground.

If she doesn't have the self-awareness to realize that she competes in her interactions, she won't even know how to make this power work against her. The desire to beat other people would impair her ability to accomplish strategic goals and eventually degrade the consistency of the relationships she hopes to rely upon.

If she improves her emotional intelligence skills, she will ensure that any contact with her colleagues strengthens her vision and a willingness to learn by igniting their enthusiasm and dedication.

Act together on your strengths and EQ:

For someone wishing to distinguish himself in his profession, skills and emotional intelligence are a dynamite mix. In the beginning, you will define your top five strengths and concentrate on improving each. First, assess your current level of EQ skills and use emotional intelligence techniques to increase your overall EQ score.

CHAPTER 20

Emotional Intelligence to Manipulate And Read A Person Like A Book

People feel nobody knows them the way they do. People say that they know their houses better than anyone else. They say that they have a much better understanding of their neighborhood than others.

People only want to pretend to understand their lives. The reality, on the other hand, is somewhat contradictory to what is claimed regarding emotions and personalities. We want to believe we are well aware of our emotions and attitudes, but the fact is that most people overlook their shortcomings.

Let's take emotional intelligence, for example. When a person becomes acquainted without much hesitation with the meaning of IT, he starts living in people who he feels have no emotional intelligence.

In reality, not many people find it difficult to look at themselves and see if they have no EI. for this purpose, an individual needs intelligence testing. Now, a person should clearly understand how much emotional intelligence shapes his or her life. The only way to make anyone understand their weaknesses is to make them aware of them.

If someone just came near you and said that you had no EI, would you consider it as true?

An individual must be given proof of his shortcomings before he is persuaded. The benefit of emotional intelligence assessments is that these assessments allow you to validate that you are correct in evaluating yourself. By going through an emotional intelligence test, you will open yourself to the possibility that you don't know what you think you are doing.

This change in appraisal makes it easier for you to adjust your way of thinking to make you more mindful of the need for further change.

Another advantage of measuring emotional intelligence is that it helps a person to accurately classify the specific part of emotional intelligence that he needs. Furthermore, these assessments make it possible for someone to grasp the potential of emotional intelligence. Through these EI tests, a person can discover how emotional intelligence is utilized every day of his life. As a result, a person can lead a much happier and prosperous life.

Besides, emotional intelligence assessments will also shed light on the degree to which they can communicate with others. Now, the social interface in one's life will prove incredibly valuable. This is dead right. You may be an employee or a student, but you certainly need someone to hold your hand as you go through the way of life.

Emotional intelligence assessments will help you develop your ability to understand other people. This skill helps you to interact with your surroundings.

Vision is the cornerstone of understanding.

If you can gain knowledge of the person's feelings, you should have no trouble counting him as part of the inner circle. Emotional intelligence testing is good because it helps a person to analyze the facts. It is common knowledge that in oneself is the greatest obstacle to the facts. An emotional intelligence test will negotiate a person's resistance and allow him to evaluate himself without harm.

CHAPTER 21

The Art of Body Language

The most beloved mode of nonverbal communication is body language. How could it be?

Well, the reply is very quick. How can anyone appreciate anything they don't understand or know how to use? Now I will probably get a lot of e-mails telling me how wrong this is, but it's far away.

Answer a question before you log in to your account. Which gender utilizes body language and all its forms the most? The answer is women. If they use it more often than men, they possibly will have a stronger body language.

Our eyes are a key instrument for the initiation of body language, usually accompanied by subtle face movements. This is why men appear to be smarter than women. On the other hand, women use all body language types. Not to say males don't, but it's not as frequent as in women.

Women are body language trainers. The form of body language used by women depends on the individual woman's personality. Shy and quiet women typically use subtler types of body language, stopping a man from knowing whether or not body language is used.

With these women, the initial readings are difficult. An outgoing and playful woman is not discreet in the use of body language at all.

They use it more openly and you will quickly note it. With their non- verbal contact, they can intensify into a little caress.

As I said it, I will clarify the use of a light touch briefly. This touch sends signals in a man's brain to receptors, which activate euphoric neurotransmitters.

The man feels a feeling of pleasure, ease, acceptability, and desires all in one, hence the euphoric situation. The trick is that you want more of it and therefore reduce this mild caress. Not enough, but not too little, to make them feel embarrassed.

What are the principal methods a woman has to display body language?

This is similar to me when I ask someone how to calculate the net value of an item. The first response is your money. The same is true of women and their use of body language but it is far from the only thing they use.

How do women use their body? One effective way is to expose a little skin. Men go nuts mentally, seeing a little skin. However, everything must also be moderately applied.

Too much exposed skin can be considered a desire for attention, where too little can be seen as close. The following are a few ways in which women use body language:

1)   The contour of the body

Women who use this typically have a stunning, voluptuous body. They use their body contours to say how they feel. They attempt to increase the ark of their bodies to improve their effects on the person they are searching for. I like this personally, as it demonstrates the natural elegance of a woman's body, close to that of a sculpture.

Why did I begin with the body? Studies suggest that the first judgment a male passes on a female without looking at facial characteristics is the body. Normally, if they don't like what they see, they move to the next woman, but if they do, they move to the other parts such as the breasts and the back.

Ladies, if I say "if they do not like what they see" this isn't about the body type. Multiple men have different types, so if you don't match your criteria, you move on. My theory is that every woman is special and it takes the right person to find them.

2)   Body Location

Typically, if women are self-confident, they use what they consider as the greatest asset they have. They can use their breast, backside or even legs. Now it all depends on the man's choice. Some men prefer one asset over the other and may decide whether he has an interest in your body language.

Women who like flaunting their breasts wear low-cut tops, those who like flaunting their backside wear tighter jeans. Those who like flaunting their thighs wear a kind of skirt. Just to prove a point, go to a Moxie, Keg, or some bar-lounger atmosphere the next time you go for lunch with some friends.

Guess what all the cocktail waitress do?

They flaunt all three of the above parts. Could you imagine their key clients? What a treat, MALES!

Just a short reality. These cocktail waitresses can have up to 5 times as many tips as a waitress in a comparable restaurant. I know these are wild phenomena. This is the biggest challenge I see when I support people in their company or love life. People look for the unobvious, I always tell them to start with the things they know or the things they have.

It's a whole different ball game for guys. You'll never see them skin- flaunting except on the beach or attempt to make body movements because men's bodies have not been designed to do that.

Men use their eye language primarily for non-verbal communication. The difference here however is whether the man dares to initiate or return non-verbal contact. Firstly, many men usually lack trust, so it isn't shocking in itself.

The key reason why men don't start with body language is that they are not secure in knowing it or how to give it back. But, if they are under the influence of alcohol, which improves instant trust, they would shy away. So ladies, if a man doesn't exhibit non-verbal communication, don't be shocked, because he has no idea what he's doing.

But when you find a man who doesn't show it but is horrendous, give him an opportunity because it's easy to repair. It is easier to teach a man the body language than to teach him how to trust.

Think of yourself as a teacher, therefore, and you teach your pupil, the guy, how to speak the right language. It also lets the man learn what to look for in the future and not be as ignorant.

As you may have observed, I move progressively towards actual initiation or what I call the "engagement" of a person to whom you are attracted, regardless of whether it is their physical appearance or perception.

It is important to do that step by step since many people say "how- to" while selling dating advice. But the dating world is so unpredictable because, as I said in front of each case, the trends shown are special, but they are eternal.

A person selling a product would have begun with an individual's initiation. But how can you do this without first knowing how you act and what you do to prove that you are interested? It's Big; this small aspect is like fishing without bait.

CHAPTER 22

Body Language to Get Something Out Of Any Circumstance

One of the most important ways of communication that we use everyday is our non-verbal or body language. It's the mode of communication that ignites our emotions and answers at the "gut- level."

Research has shown that knowing one's body language improves one's desire to get something out of any circumstance.

Have you ever seen a couple sit together and had a sense about how good or bad their relationship was in minutes?

Have you ever wondered how easily you could draw this conclusion without direct interaction?

Whether you know this or not, we spend our days listening to people's non-verbal signs in their body language and drawing conclusions from our observations.

Our body language shows the reality that we conceal from the world, like how we feel, our relationships, and our circumstances.

Through our eyes, movements, body location and face, the people with whom we communicate will assess our intentions, our relationship content, the degree of superiority we have in any given situation, our level of trust and our true motives and desires.

The intensity of the body language is found in its emotional response. In nearly every situation, emotions influence decisions and reactions. Non-verbal signals activate emotions that define a person's core assets, such as truthfulness, integrity, fairness, ability, and leadership skills. The perception of these signs will decide who we date, the job in which we are working, how good we are and who can be elected to important political positions.

Why do we not spend years studying and improving successful body language skills for such an essential skill?

The fact is that most people underestimate the value of body language before they pursue a deeper definition of human conduct in a personal relationship or gain a foothold in a competitive business situation.

Mastery of body language offers people the keys to understand the meaning behind certain movements and body movement and to understand how thoughts can be efficiently conveyed and expressed while communicating with others.

This dramatically increases the overall efficacy of interpersonal relationships.

The best way to begin this learning process is to learn the fundamental understanding of the two main styles of body language – the open presence and closed presence.

The closed presence body language style is seen in people who fold their bodies around the central lines of the body, which extend from the top of their heads to their feet.

The physical features that make up this kind of appearance are feet closely together. Arms are placed near to the body and hands are crossed or placed together in front of the body. Little hand movements are kept close to the body.

The signals transmitted to the world by the form of the body language of the closed presence are lack of trust, low self- confidence, impotence, and lack of experience. In extreme cases, the message that you want to be invisible may also be produced. The consequences on the individual projectors of this form of language may range from not getting the best possibilities to a worst-case scenario for the self-fulfillment of victimization.

The open presence, by comparison, is present in people who build a sense of authority, power, and leadership by projecting trust, achievement, strength and skills.

The physical attributes of the feet are casual, open hand movements used in conversations along the middle line of the body, elbows keeping them away from the body, shoulders keeping them behind, straight stances and eyes fixed on the level of the audience.

These people are seen as beautiful, ambitious, intelligent and efficient. We regard this form of body language as the "body language of leaders."

To develop body language and begin to project an open presence, eye contact is essential. Eye contact is one of our core communication methods. When you communicate with others, you will alter the way others see them. When people start speaking directly in the eyes of an individual, they are seen as confident, reliable and competent.

Hand movements and facial expressions are the second degree of transition that can be displayed freely. These modes of communication improve the ability to convey information effectively and efficiently. By using open hand motions away from the individual and expressively manipulating the face, the greater impact is produced by the visual awareness of the listener and the amount of information presented during the interaction.

As youngsters, we are taught from a young age that good boys and girls sit together properly with the legs and the hands folded before them. Encouraging children to restrict their physical space may establish some of the features of a closed adult presence in the body language.

To counter this influence, the features of the open presence body language can be adopted and integrated into its natural state of being. If this transition in conduct is achieved, it offers the same non- verbal experiences and signals as its transparent counterparts.

Awareness of body language is necessary if the most successful presentation is to be achieved in all interpersonal interactions. Individuals lacking this knowledge are vulnerable to confusion and struggle to express their ideas. With the ability to distinguish between various body language styles, anyone can acquire the skills required to excel in any mission it chooses.

CHAPTER 23

---◇◇◇---

Understand Your Body Language For Defense Against Manipulation

Whether you are aware of it or not, your body language is a major factor in how you approach others. Listening skills are a must and very important for developing good relationships with clients in many careers, particularly those in which you support others.

Whether you help people to improve their ties, provide people with feedback for business success, or advise on some other issue, they see your body language and show strong listening skills. It makes people more relaxed.

Poor body language could cause you to lose something wonderful. Your body language can make others feel important as you give them the attention they need.

On the other hand, it is important to know the symptoms of the bad listener and try to get rid of them. You don't want to hear what he or she is doing. This most definitely would lead to the end of the relationship which may lead to major business losses.

So what can you do to start sending positive signals to the person with whom you speak?

At the time of contact, we come to the body position. You need to take an open position. You must never hold your arms or legs close or the other person will think you don't want to hear his point.

If you lean forward when talking to others, the body language suggests that you are paying more attention to what he or she is doing. In comparison, leaning away means you don't have much interest at all.

Communication with the eye is the most significant aspect. Try to keep the eye in contact at all times. If you continue to look or look away, it shows that you have little interest in the matter and that you feel awkward. Furthermore, the value of a relaxed stance cannot be overlooked. Don't try to be too rigid.

You shouldn't be too formal to speak to anyone either. If you believe your body has experienced significant losses in the past, you should start following the aforementioned tips immediately.

Body Language Talks All the time:

The moment you leave your house, your body language starts to speak for you. Even though you don't talk, while you're standing, sitting, and using your hands, that's what some see as a contact.

So if you have no good knowledge of body language, often your language will not correspond to what your purposes are and people will get the wrong message. If your body language is inconsistent with what your motives are, you will lose your reputation.

How to maintain credibility

So, what can you do to preserve your credibility? We should learn a bit more about body language, be more trustworthy and professional in others' eyes. Make your entry as good as possible when you reach your customer for any form of company.

How can you do that?

You can start by talking about the company once you reach the customer's premises. Taking papers or checking the case gives a negative message. Even if you have to wait a while, instead, you can read any magazine.

Another significant lesson in body language is to shake hands warmly and firmly. We come next to the selection of the chair to sit on. You should never say that you would just sit when the other person asks you.

Instead, pick the most suitable chair and sit right away. Never make the mistake of sitting too near or too far from the customer. How much room you can hold depends on the customer's personality. A shy person needs to sit a little more than an outgoing person. The optimal size, however, is between 20 and 50 inches. You can lean towards the consumer if you try to emphasize a certain argument.

Importance of Eye and Voice Contact:

Another important aspect of body language is eye contact. Communication with your eyes and a smile on your face will show you as being true, sincere and transparent. Slight eye contact and a glance here and there will always give you the message that you don't have enough confidence.

But also stop continually looking at the other person, as this makes the consumer feel very awkward. Try to talk in your normal voice still. If your voice is enthusiastic, it will quickly take the customer's attention.

Body language: what are the different postures?

You should consider your body language to be outstanding when you speak in your usual tone and when the volume is also regular.

A well-modulated voice with a regular rhythm and pace shows interest and passion. The words you use during your speech should be as simple as possible. On the other hand, when you use 'um' or 'a' or clear your throat excessively, then it sends out a message that you are nervous.

Emphasis on Posture and Manipulation

You should also concentrate on your movements and postures if you want to improve your body language. Here are some easy suggestions for enhancing posture. You should always walk freely, take fast, fixed steps with swinging arms, but you should stand upright.

If you hold the other person's eye in contact, cup your chin between your finger and thumb, or cross the nose bridge with your hands or reach the chin, then you show that you are thinking about what is said.

Some negative indicators of body language

On the contrary, bad body language involves anxious gestures that suggest carelessness. In reality, all you have to do is to stop looking nervous and keep yourself aware of your body language message.

For example, when you fold your arms, cross the legs, try to catch lint that is not on your skin, or shift your hands on the face, you express your disagreement with that of the others.

Blinking your eyes repeatedly, coughing multiple times, looking at the time of the conversation and seeing various locations by rapidly moving your eyes indicate negative behavior.

Frustration

If you point at something with your index finger, you'll demonstrate your anger with your body language. Similarly, wringing your mouth, playing with the hair and tightly clamping your mouth are signs of anger. Now, how can someone prove that he's bored?

If the listener's eyes aren't fixed on the person who talks, whether he is distracted or if he's interested to do anything more than listen to what is said, he shows that he's getting bored. The value of body language increases even more when you encounter people from different cultures.

The Importance of Body Language

Language is the most critical part of what we communicate. It is usually more reliable than words we use. I will share some explanations for the value of body language, and then give you a short quiz to see how well you understand its meaning.

Some of the things we say about our bodies will help us to improve why we say it. When simply saying "I don't know," the following movements have little to add. We should turn our hands face up in front of us by lifting our brows and turning our eyes, while slightly gripping our bottom lip and looking sideways. Now we have made someone laugh and maybe lifted a little of the burden off ourselves or the other guy, who was a little worried that we didn't know something we didn't know.

Furthermore, paying attention to the body language of someone will help us determine when someone does not tell us the truth. Here are some signs that someone might lie. Sometimes a person who does not know the truth would not want to make contact with the eye because the eyes are windows to his lying souls.

There are, however, other signs of deceit. A person who does not speak the full truth will clear his throat, stump or change his or her voice as though trying to distract attention from his or her lie or to pause, so they can think of a valid response or plausible explanation.

Moreover, taps or bounces, blush, place your hand on your forehead, turn away or raise your shoulders may all mean that you don't have a conversation and you don't know the truth.

Another essential feature of corporal language is to communicate our thoughts on what we speak on. The body language will help us decide how someone thinks about what they say.

An individual, for example, might tell her boss that she is happy to take the matter into account but her body language may show that she is not happy about it. This can be an essential move that can help a manager decide who the right person to do this role is.

In a work interview, body language may be the deciding factor. If the applicant's corporate language indicates he is comfortable with the subject matter and has faith, he is more likely to get the job, particularly in this harsh job market. We spoke earlier that some body language is considered tense and out of reach. These are some of the same features that make a job seeker less confident and relaxed.

In a relationship, one's body language may show that one pays attention or doesn't care what the other person says. Moving towards the discussion demonstrates that the person needs to hear what the other person says. Leaning back will prove he was unselfish or thought superior.

Reaching forward and standing near during conversation can mean that someone is actively trying to convince or control the conversation. When you hear someone without eye contact, you don't pay attention but wait for your chance to speak. This gives your friend the impression that it doesn't matter what they say and they won't listen closely to you when it's up to you to speak.

CHAPTER 24

———————— ✺ ————————

Body Language Secrets To Get What You Want

Body language is an important tool that can affect our thought and decisions. If used skillfully, others can be manipulated and made to think and respond as you wish them to behave by the strategic projection of your deliberate body movements, facial expressions, and gestures.

The creation of good clues and the avoidance of a few easy pitfalls are best for you in two basic ways:

1.   When you use positive body language, you can look and feel more confident. If you step and take yourself confidently and tend to "project" positive vibes, you feel more relaxed and controlled instantly.

2.   Relation of the body language is contagious. In the speech, we appear to imitate each other. Have you noticed how we tend to fit the speaking tone, actions, gestures and facial expressions of the other person?

It's not great when we talk everyday and without understanding it. When using positive body language, it is more likely that the other person uses positive body language (mirror you), which in turn makes the other person feel those emotions (happier or trust in his decisions, etc.).

Caution: The same is also valid if the actions of the body's language, facial expressions, or gestures are negative, even if your intention is not to do so.

We recognize that the use of constructive body language improves the mood of everyone. Notice how a stand-up comic can make an audience laugh with gestures, facial expressions and body movements. The verbal message is always humorous but the body language amplifies the laughter and the reaction of the audience.

Here are some ways to communicate easier without using words:

1.   Pay attention to your encouraging signs.

a.   Allow direct eye contact as much as possible. In North America and the United Kingdom, about 70% is acceptable. In Japan, for instance, the acceptable 'gas rate' is close to 50% and the acceptable 'gas rate' will grow to 90% in most Scandinavian countries. Realize that cultural variations are one of three keys to the understanding of body language.

b.   Smile with your lips or relax. Stop pursing your lips or constantly scratching your ears. Nobody trusts someone who constantly touches his face while talking.

c.   Stand with a free stance. Keep the arms and legs loose and comfortable and either stand at a slight angle to the other person or to the right eye while facing the other person. Looking at the other person's left eye is most convenient to talk or hear.

d.   Hold your palms facing up and keep your hands relaxed. It is important to show the open palm more often when you gesture. This alerts the unconscious mind that you are not dangerous.

e.   Stop nervous or fidgeting motions like clicking your nails or adjusting your jingling. This suggests a high degree of "internal dialogue" or "self chatter." You can project fear, restlessness and nervousness or just want to get going.

2.   Pay close attention to the other person's body language when maintaining dialogue. Check for negative language signs or indicators that the consumer is bored. The other person may start looking over your shoulder, play on the jacket with the button, jingle keys and preen with various articles like scarves, mitts and caps.

3.   Subtly begin to mimic the body language of the other person.

You should lean forward to demonstrate interest if the customer leans forward. If your arms are crossed, you still cross the arms but show your fingers to make sure they are spread out.

Once you are in touch, start leading. Test to see if you are willing to lead. For example, if you dine with others, reach for your glass of water. If they too meet and follow you, you are now in touch!

4. If you want a more optimistic tone in the conversation, change your body language slowly to be more optimistic. Uncross your arms and legs, slightly turn your head when you hear and straighten your back when you speak. When talking to a tilted head in the company,

nobody is taken seriously. (Note: The head tilt works well or is incredibly effective when dating or flirting!)

5. The following is important to remember. Try to not change your body language (excessive body move, face touch, tense knee motion) when you start speaking, as this usually means that you are attempting to regulate the conversation.

When possible, during a pause, you can move, relax in your stance and then start talking.

In short, be careful to monitor your body language strategically and observe the reactions of others. You will start to understand how powerful it is to use your own body strategically to target the other person and to get the desired result. You would be shocked at how easy it is to get what you want without a word!

CHAPTER 25

Why We Get Confused with Body Language and Attraction

Body language experts inform us that our knowledge of non-verbal communication will build relationships and strengthen our impact. Sounds nice, but is that true? Why do so many of us still find it very difficult to understand the body language of men/women?

This is what the study of modern communication about body language has to say:

1.   Not all a man or woman does to his/her body is a message or a warning

Some ordinary movements used by both males and females may look like those of the language of flirtation or seduction, although certain movements and expressions may not be used to flirt and seduce. The body language such as smiling, lip-licking, gaze-holding tucking hair, head-cocking, quick-eye blinks, personal touching, etc. can be more ingrained personal patterns than flicking or "come-ons."

2.   The limitless connection between expression and emotion makes it difficult to understand what emotion is expressed.

Even the smile that we are all conscious of will also mask a range of emotions. We might look at a person and say, "Oh, he or she is smiling. He or she must be happy," and we may or may not know correctly the emotion that comes from pleasure, courteous salutation, frustration, fear, disappointment, uncertainty, excuse, sarcasm or disdain.

3. It is always a fair chance that some of the emotions we read from the body language of a person are a product based on our interpretation of reality, experiences, expectations, and beliefs that can have nothing to do with others ...

When we find that the facial expressions or movements of our date are not compatible with our interpretation of emotions or movements, we make a negative evaluation of the individual. However, the emotion we assigned to the face or gesture may not have been what the sender intended to do. If you have a "positive" body language, but if the other person, for instance, is in an offensive or hostile state, you can perceive the gesture as aggression or abuse.

4. Contrary to what most of us believe, body language, both consciously and subconsciously, can be influenced and controlled. For example, anyone who knows that people believe that those who lie cannot look into the eye can master the "honest trait" of looking into the eyes of others and can fool anyone who is based on that single conviction.

If you know that a hug demonstrates affection, you will knowingly hug your worst enemy with a smile.

5. The way we use and understand body language depends on where we come from ...

Research shows that we appear to be more adaptive and able to notice changes in people's body language relative to our own social,

cultural and educational contexts as well as the size of their body, age, gender, etc.

So, what do I want to say? To be informed about the signs of interest between men and women, do not read too many body language signs. Smilers, nodders and fakers will play you in the process of rejection, so do not expect too long for such non-verbal signs to be given.

Don't spend much time studying their body language as they are sometimes not predictive, as mentioned above. We ask for clarification when using words, but in the body language, we cannot ask others to repeat it when it is not understood. Furthermore, we can't say "wrong" and start again, if we find ourselves using the "just a minute" body language.

The method I am teaching and writing about is very easy as it is focused on tuning into the individual energy or sex vibrations of a particular person and involving that person in his or her vibration. It's like talking to someone who uses their emotional language.

It transmits acceptance and openness that in turn makes it more relaxed, producing for you both a meaningful and enjoyable experience. When the emotional interaction of this nature arises, you both think and feel emotionally connected.

CHAPTER 26

The Gentle Art of Persuasion

Why does one person change our entire mental attitude so easily and make us do what we had no idea about doing just an hour ago?

Why would one person persuade us we should purchase a product (or service) that we were sure a few minutes ago we didn't need it or would not buy it under any circumstances?

Because he/she is a master of subtle persuasion.

How little we know how much persuasion plays in our lives. The academic, the lawyer, the entrepreneur, the salesman, the parent, each of them seeks to convince, control, win over others their way of thinking, their values, and to embrace their ideas. Nothing more significant than persuasion is among the many elements that come into a scientific approach to sale.

My insurance friend, Ed, also finds the mind of a prospect utterly opposed to him. The consumer does not want to purchase life insurance, or at least he does not think he needs to buy it. He rejects any chance of persuasion and is motivated to do what he has chosen not to do.

But a little later, he happily buys his family's insurance, he pays for it and he is sure he needs it. The mindset of thecustomer has been modified by the art of convincing and winning over, all achieved by

successive rational sale method steps, which must be done in order to result in sales.

The first move was to get the customer's attention; otherwise, Ed could not have done anything. This is also a difficult thing for a person who is willing to not look at your goods, who has chosen not to buy or to look at you.

But Ed is a successful sales representative who doesn't try to force a prospect to purchase until he not only secures his attention but has also taken a strong interest in his bid. He then stirs up his urge to get what he has to sell and the deal is not over until this is finished.

The whole essence of Ed was his wonderful capacity to convince people to change their minds and to look at things from his point of view. I've never met a person who's been so good at turning someone else's mind to his way of thinking. And that's the essence of marketing – the ability to make items look different as we see them.

There is a kind of hypnotic force that passes by persuasiveness, but it is not focused on integrity and seriously harms the business of an individual in the long run.

Manipulation is just a superficial road to persuasion. The manipulator is the only one who profits for the long term.

A greedy salesman often places larger orders than other sales agents in his company, but in the end, he loses customers and puts his career at risk, while the individual who does not sell so much at an early stage has a stronger relationship and keeps his customers because he seeks their interests and only tries to purchase them to his advantage.

If you want success, you need to consider the needs and desires of your customer, and that is how you gain trust in yourself and the product you are selling.

The opportunity to make someone think as you do is immense power and a massive responsibility. If not honestly working, it will prove to be a boomerang and harm customers. You will soon be identified as a manipulator and people are not going to work with you. If he has a small hint of you manipulating him, or whether he sees the slightest signs of insincerity, your time is running out.

We first must trust in the honesty of an individual, even if he can manipulate us before he can convince us to do what we didn't think we would do. The typical businessman needs hard facts today.

But salesmen with compelling powers should present these facts in such a way that the possibility of the salesperson being his friend is made to work fully for him. Nobody likes the idea of being "managed," and no matter how much he likes flattery, if you try, he will ask you why.

Know your prospects can be on his guard against some form of persuasion. He will look for insincerity proof. He does not wish to be tricked or exploited. Most importantly, note that honesty is no substitute in any region.

CHAPTER 27

Persuasion Science for Exploring Human Influence

Success in every area of life needs other people's cooperation. If our definition of success means joining a certain university, having a certain job, or marrying the special individual and bringing up a family, we still need the support of others. It is therefore important for us to learn how to successfully manipulate people to convince them to help us achieve our goals.

Contemplating the topic of persuasion and power can initially make some people feel uncomfortable. Maybe it seems like this subject is the world of deceptive or manipulative people.

Do we have to use people in the study of persuasion and influence?

Should we use illegal or unethical methods to advance our own lives?

None of these questions have any basis. Although scrupulous people will often try to deceive and exploit others, the science of persuasion in its purest form aims to produce a beneficial outcome for all concerned.

Even if there are some strong concerns about learning how we affect others, we can still be influenced by others. We do this by our perceptions, our appearance, voice, body language and actions.

Persuasion science provides a clear picture of how relationships with others affect people. At any point in our lives, learning these concepts of human interaction can be dramatic.

Even as a youth, we are easily engulfed in the domain of power and conviction. Our parents are trying to encourage us to take these first steps, consume certain foods, and follow certain codes of conduct. We are introduced to the idea of peer pressure, where certain children control their peers strongly in the same setting, while other children are pressured to pursue a desired course of action.

In many advertising outlets, we are subject to media control and persuasion, and we are trying to influence the opinion of the opposite sex as we enter the everyday life process. Our applications and letters of recommendation are aimed at persuading people to grant us admission to our university of choice.

Job interviews also affect a prospective employer and convince him to offer us a role.

When we are looking for success in our professions, they use the same criteria to reassure our bosses that we are deserving of promotions and pay increases.

The life cycle is completed by trying to reassure our children and influence them in various ways, including their actions and academic success.

Which parent wouldn't want to know how to avoid and motivate their children efficiently?

It is probably evident at this stage that our lives are affected and convinced and it is a topic that has been recognized as a science.

A lot of research has been done on the human mind and the effect of our actions on our climate.

If we grasp these values, we will achieve in life even better than if we were unaware of them. Besides, a deep understanding of the essential principles of persuasion can also be a strong defense against the unscrupulous people in our lives who can try to deceive or exploit us.

Influence and persuasion have gone from the art of vendors and politicians to a science focused on vast research.

However, while most entrepreneurs understand the underlying concepts of persuasion, they nevertheless strive to use them effectively.

Why?

'Calvin and Hobbes' (Jim Waterson) Calvin-a little boy- is watching advertisements on TV in one of the favorite pictures from the comic strip. He stares at the computer and says, "Manipulate me!"

Unfortunately, most people are wrong to speak to Calvin. Naturally, the opposite is true. Perhaps they don't want to be affected. Surely, they don't want to be exploited.

The element of control

It doesn't work to hypnotize someone who doesn't want to be hypnotized. Not all the worldwide hypnotherapy methods can succeed. The same is true of power. You need to determine their influence before you attempt to influence others. This is not gullibility or malevolence – they need to be affected.

Because of the situation and the individual, we all experience times when we want to be influenced. I want it to affect my mood when I go to the movies to see a comedy. I want them to affect my thought if I pay to see one of my heroes deliver a speech.

When I buy a book called 'How to suit,' I want it to affect my actions. And sometimes we are glad to be affected-sometimes exploited. When I go to my favorite masseuse, I lie on the bench thinking, "Manipulate me!" I know it makes me feel better and I can't function if I fight it.

Calendar

Because of timing, most efforts to influence and convince others usually fail. They're just not ready. It's like trying to entice someone when they aren't hungry in your restaurant. Nobody would like to be affected before these two questions are answered.

1. Do they know what you're talking about? Intelligent people are always ready to listen to reliable experts, particularly if they are given insights that improve their understanding of a particular problem.

2. What do they try to accomplish? If I think you want me to conclude that you will profit most of all, then any effort to convince me will be resisted. If I believe you want to help me make the right decision more easily, I am highly influential.

Prepare the soil

Every farmer knows that before a seed can take root, you have to prepare the soil.

As an influencer, you have to 'prepare the land' before you try:

1. Establish your reputation by giving them insights into your field of knowledge that improve your understanding. It may clarify some confusing terminology, correct common mistaken assumptions, or suggest some emerging trends.

2.   Inform them of your intention. Your task should be to help them analyze the data, define options, and prioritize questions to achieve the best result. Ideally, you will be the 'facilitator of decision.' Recognizing how difficult it is to make a decision today in the world, your goal is to encourage them to decide confidently.

3.   Make the similarities obvious. If I think you can understand me, I'm more likely to be swayed by what you say. When I see we have similar life conditions, interests, preferences, and tastes, it is only natural that you can more easily sympathize with me. Research has shown that a higher percentage of settlements later rewards time spent building common ground.

4.   Prepare your social facts. Some people will never be swayed by you, especially on long-standing beliefs. However, they may be affected by their acts as analogous to them. Prepare a variety of potential points of reference and use your introductory discussion to determine which ones are of the greatest importance to them.

The chance of failure

If you have attempted to manipulate me unsuccessfully in the past, the next time you will find it harder. Your efforts to impact must therefore be given the greatest chance of success. Assess the effect of the other. See if it is poor and decide what you can do with the above points to improve it. It's safer to postpone it before you lose your energy and risk losing the relationship.

Persuasion science has tremendous potential, but only when the receiver is ready and it is understood.

CHAPTER 28

— ∽ —

Manipulation and Persuasion In Daily Life

Health practitioners have expressed concerns about the lack of nutrition awareness in the community in recent years. Could this be one explanation for the many food shows on TV now?

How much can we be convinced of what we see on a small screen?

Are we treated in our choice of foods and qualified in nutrition without being fully aware of it?

There is no denying that manipulation was a factor when people took control over others. -- The waking moment is controlled with a bombardment of ads, fact, and opinion, so that we fulfill the needs and wishes of the advertiser.

Right now, I try to convince you, which is a form of manipulation, to bear witness to my view. The art of persuasion is a part of life. While we engage in a normal conversation, we use this type.

Manipulation or conviction

Very often we don't even know that we are being manipulated until we know that our attitude or ideas about a subject are shifting. Our protections were not in place and we possibly did not realize the evolving type of conviction that was directed at us.

I am convinced to listen to your opinions and can actively determine whether I agree or whether I have a different opinion. But, if I get influenced, then it is more possible that I do not understand the shift in attitude that is being implemented.

If I am not aware, for example, that Margaret Fulton had agreed to launch a Woolworth initiative, her assertion that Matt Preston was more showman than a chef may have inspired me but, understanding that she might have had competing priorities in her hit, the effect of her statement on me might have diminished.

We are often affected by advertisements, perception, and even debates, and the manipulation of our thought is always difficult to see. We like to think that we regulate our emotions, but are we?

Sometimes there are secret agendas, and it is a consciousness of those forces which enable us to be willing or unwilling pawns in life.

I have taught sales and customer service at a nearby technical college for over ten years. Inevitably, my class and I are having long talks on sales ethics, the value of sales; how the sales process in all cases is used; why sales have such a bad name and why good salesmen aren't only paid liars.

Our discussions typically come back to one basic definition. Persuasion is just a fancy term for manipulation without honesty. If the distinction is not clear:

Manipulation means making people feel guilty for their success and happiness, making people do something that they don't want to do, make people believe in lies and do things that way, and make people feel inferior because they look at the world in the way they do.

Manipulators use people's feelings against them and lose trust in them. Manipulation is used because they have nothing else to offer.

Conversely, persuasion seeks to show people their achievement and satisfaction. Persuasion aims to encourage people to find the strength they need to do, to consider the implications of their actions and to decide wisely on their decisions.

People are convinced that it allows them to explain what they have to say in terms that others can easily absorb.

Persuasion allows you to clearly hear equally from another, overly emotional person. It remains their preference whether or not people want to consume what you have to say. You can never refuse people the freedom to choose for themselves. Your success in influencing others depends largely on how much you appreciate your bid. The more you sell them, the more they enjoy. Keep this in mind as you try to convince yourself in your life.

CHAPTER 29

***

The Art of Positive Persuasion

If you want to excel in 2020and beyond, unleash the sales giant you've ever seen, as you step away from old schools of thoughts and concentrate on positive influence and persuasion, to create meaningful, mutually beneficial relationships with those who are right to sell.

But I think it's reasonable to say that you would have the same sales potential if you are in sales. I will help you unlock your sales giant and help you meet all of your sales goals this year with this chapter.

If you want to succeed in sales, you will need to have the best interest in your customers and prospects.

This ensures that you will never generate profits in the long run if you try to influence or threaten customers, instead of affecting them positively.

Understanding the idea of positive impact

Starting point: to affect others positively, you need to recognize that there are three different sections to be convinced.

Logical

The first involves the use of logic, i.e. this is a method in which you fully understand the value offer and the right person who needs exactly what you need to give. To inform them using this knowledge, you encourage them to use their reasoning to come to a positive conclusion where they fully understand your proposition of value and agree that it meets or exceeds their needs and expectations.

Emotion

As you know, people buy through their feelings; you must recognize this main element in the process of persuasion. This is the part of the sales process that you must addressed and ensure your customer has grasped all the logical reasons why your product or service is the best option.

You completely understand your proposition of value from a logical perspective at this point. Your job now as a salesperson is to appeal to the positive emotions of your customers so that they can understand "What is in it for them." The positive emotions I am talking about here are pleasure, happiness, significant achievement, appreciation, affection, compassion, respect, and pride.

You need to truly understand the value proposition and all the advantages it gives the customer to make this aspect of the sales process work for you. From this point of view, discover how your customers can benefit from using your product or service and explain it emotionally.

Idea: Explore the optimistic emotions mentioned above, now investigate the advantages of your product or service. Link your customers to one or more of the advantages your product provides and explain to them one of the positive feelings they can feel when your product or service is being used.

Legal problems

The final rod of moral faith is honesty, continuity and good character. Essentially, for a good sales professional, it means that they must always be genuine, 100% truthful and believe entirely in what they have to offer.

The truly great sales professional believes not only in what they sell and do but is a living example. Their acts, words and deeds reflect what they say. In other words, you must speak to yourself if you want to be a successful sales professional. You want the world to seeyou as an example. You will never try to convince someone positively if you are not able to do so.

Much like you would never ask anyone to do or never do anything; you cannot establish a mutually beneficial long-term business relationship with someone if you want to sell anything you wouldn't want.

Your customers will see through you if you seek to sell them something that you don't 100% believe in. People are very sensitive to feelings and can easily detect your negative feelings in the word or body language while discussing your product. The trick to being successful when influencing people positively is to be 100% honest and genuine. If you pretend to be something you are not, people will see through you. Being truthful and ethical is the exact opposite of deceit when persuading people.

If you are a living example of your selling pitch and people can see that you care for your best interests, they can warm up to you easily

and build long-term relationships with you. What do you expect? Be honest and ethical and this year will open the doors to your sales success.

CHAPTER 30

Efficient Persuasion Strategies With No Manipulation Feeling

In this chapter, I will be sharing some genuine ways to fire your mind and do something for yourself without making you feel bound. Generally speaking, the preference of people differs according to two different methods, manipulation and persuasion.

All of us want to succeed in persuading others to have the same view, approve or do something for us.

What is the fine line between belief and manipulation?

What are the motivational strategies so that you learn to manipulate others rather than dominate their decisions?

Persuading others is a way to imply that you have to get what you want or force someone to do something for you. Manipulating is a way of deceiving people by misleading methods only to force them to do what you want.

The discrepancy between persuasion and manipulation may be exacerbated by the intent of the attacker.

And the most truthful way should be to excel in voicing your wishes without being deceptive.

Here are some effective persuasion methods without a sense of manipulation:

Make sure you first know what you want and then verbalize it. You should let other people know your interests, ambitions, and thoughts. Speak your mind ... How can anyone know what you want if you don't even know it?

For example, if you always wanted a birthday party, let other people know that you're pleased with this. Speak up and share your suggestions. Secondly, we know that our friends and family represent us. If you're not a nice guy, your friends probably won't be like that.

Learn how to listen to what your friends say and whether they want or need to talk. Review your skills to see if you can do more to help. Then, if it calls for something, they can be convinced to phone in and do something for you.

Instead, strive not to be a sort of friend who often asks for support or benefits. Try to socialize with your peers, make something out of yourself and exchange skills with each other. Therefore, you will build a better bond that allows you the freedom to be yourself and not be someone else.

Third, don't be afraid to say other people's good words or deeds. One explanation why some of us hesitate or postpone to help others is because they feel their gift is just unsatisfactory.

If you are a fussy person and you are too hard to please, others will be too reluctant to help you solve any problems.

Try not to be a person who is always sad and needs to see it just so, that's the way you can be a nice person and not greedy to say sweet words and gratitude. Next time, if somebody gives you a small gift or

someone helps, try to send them a Thank You card or just tell them you appreciated it. It goes a long way to have a thankful heart.

Last but not least, don't isolate yourself from others. We do need the support of others in practical terms.

Life isn't a bed of roses. Most of our day is so stressful, distressing and frustrating, but a warm touch or just knowing that someone is by our side makes things simpler and more bearable.

However, on this downside of your life, other people hesitate to meet you and don't want to bother you, so you should get away from your course ... Pick up the phone or send an e-mail when you know you want to sit with your friends on the rollercoaster trip.

All in all, nobody can make a bridge or knock on your door to see how you are doing, but if you are used to contacting them and follow the steps above, then they will be there when you need them to do something for you.

Conviction strategies are just a matter of understanding what you want and putting them into writing.

Human nature is good and we wanted to help and we wanted to be helped.You do not know what you need or how to help but you can tell them that you don't want to be manipulated and abused.

CHAPTER 31

― ∽ ―

Improving Your Persuasion Techniques

The power of persuasion will open doors and ease the road to success. You will have a variety of compelling strategies available after reading this chapter. The most compelling strategies are based on NLP. These methods of persuasion are focused on empathy – you must consider them to convince others.

Persuasive strategies focused on empathy

The first and most important thing you need to understand is that what your mind best reacts to is sensation, visual or auditory stimulation. Knowing it will allow you to be more convincing by filling in and fulfilling this particular desire.

Women typically react best but not always to feelings. Men respond to visuals as well, and some people are influenced by audio. Look at how you speak and learn what the best stimulus is and center your persuasion.

Do you say, "I see," "I hear what you're saying" or "I feel that ..." These are obvious examples; of course, the right response may be more nuanced and maybe a combination of two stimulation styles.

The more you are aware of the person you work with, the more easily your persuasion tactics can be optimized.

Persuasive Mirror-Based Methods

Corresponding to your body language and your position is a subtle but shockingly effective convincing strategy. You need to be subtle and at first, feel awkward but with some practice, you see how efficient this technique, known as the 'mirroring' technique, can be to develop a relationship and ease persuasion.

You can also adjust your language and how you talk to focus your persuasion in a way that is well connected with your personality. People should respond to persuasive techniques in their own "language." Take those words you use and use them, in different adjectives. Be aware of their tempo, pitch, and volume and react as much as possible.

There are also other compelling methods you can practice and expand on. I recommend that you learn the most powerful strategies for empathy/persuasion. The following techniques may, however, be useful additions to your belief.

Use "now" terms like "today" or "at the moment" to indicate urgency subliminally.

Rhetorical Benches

The individual is highly motivated to think for himself and therefore can be extremely convincing. Ask questions that challenge them and they become more receptive automatically. This will also help you to learn more. This will also often persuade them to make a decision when you have already merely guided them to this conviction.

Communication

It is important to have a good relationship with the person you are trying to convince. This is almost impossible without eye contact. You may build trust with regular and non-threatening eye contact. Add a true smile and convincing will be much simpler.

Be Convinced By Personal Intelligence, Not Prejudice.

Everyone in politics would tell you that people just don't respond rationally. They respond with emotions. To convince others, you have to personally communicate with them.

The three basic elements of each compelling argument were established by Aristotle:

Ethos: the integrity, experience, intelligence, status and power of a person who attempts to convince them.

Logos: reasoning, critical thought, knowledge and evidence appeal.

Pathos: the call to emotions; non-cognitive impulses that influence decisions and behavior.

Of course, all layers are important but perhaps the emotional layer has the greatest persuasion. We are emotional creatures who are much more likely to feel good than to be convinced that something is right.

Is Technological Reasoning Ethical?

Of course, you may think it is unethical to use persuasion tactics. Indeed, you might have the dilemma of using them on someone you love. It is up to you how you feel using compelling methods but note the following. People should know whether others are attempting to exploit the techniques. If you convince someone effectively, you have out-competed them.

Conviction is still optional. After a lot of practice, however, you can find that these compelling strategies simply blend into your being. Should you feel bad for using other facets of your personality like speaking with confidence?

You can most of the time strive to do what's best for them. The aim of emotionally engaging with someone is to learn what they want. If you know this, you just convince them to do what they want to do. Therefore, persuasion is not manipulation by its name-it simply raises the argument.

People should be adequately conscious to make their own decisions. You should hopefully be assured that you can use these convincing strategies to do the best thing for those concerned.

CHAPTER 32

Ways to Overcome Manipulation by Others

Many decent people in the world can use motivational resources to support you in times of need without ever thinking a second way. In the meantime, some find it easy to exploit and use others to their benefit. They do many things to manipulate others. These ten forms and instruments of persuasion can help you know what you are doing and how you can solve it.

1: Me or you

Many manipulators are greedy, so you want to protect yourself. This also leads to alienation from friends, family and others. You learn to say no to them and prefer others while trying to choose between them and others. If they take care of you, they won't bring you there.2: I do this, you owe it to me.

The manipulators also use tactics to convince you but afterward, milk you for everything they can. If you can, even if you can, say no to their demands and don't bother with them.

3: I'm still worse than you.

These individuals are almost difficult to stop. The best bet is to avoid or disregard them only when they start with the antiquities.

4: Are you cheating yourself?

You have to find out how you exploit someone in the way you are. If so, you must first take action to eliminate it from your behavior. Looking at yourself is one of the best convincing devices.

5: Use your behavior.

One of the strongest techniques to use against the act of manipulation is to use your actions to deter the manipulators. If they believe you are strong enough to resist, they will possibly go to others.

6: Self-improvement

Recognize methods of persuasion and exit the situation before it becomes too much of a challenge. The situation can quickly become unsafe if you linger too long.

7: Record it

If someone attempts to intimidate you and you start to fear for yourself or others' protection, go to the police or an agency that specializes in violence.

8: Stop being honest

The manipulator's integrity would only provide fuel for their flames. If you are truthful about your feelings or opinions, they use manipulative techniques to turn them around and use them as a guilt trip and a stopping point.

9: Am I insane?

Sometimes, manipulators will try to make you feel stupid by saying one thing. Later they will fail to ask you about your health.

10. Tiny Helper

You always believe manipulation is a great aid but looking closely, you can see the manipulation methods you use and that you never volunteer, but you say yes to most requests. You will use this act later and self-improvement is likely to be affected by it.

CONCLUSION

Different identities in parallel worlds are formed by interactions and our consequent thought processes. Working on different premises means that we are largely unaware of our divided personalities before faced with circumstances involving a clash of wills.

Irony and battle lie not in squelching certain aspects that are unfavorable to us but in recognizing that the component of our lives we aim to preserve are the very elements that should be killed.

The danger to self is most apparent as we try to merge our spirits-for they serve different purposes. One part of us wants to live and experience life to the fullest, while the other fights to maintain a pre- determined life and way of living that is adverse to change.

I call it the "why not and who said" factor versus the "what's the point" factor.

Why not and who says – challenge our security systems at every turn and every point, try to understand where we chose to take no opportunity, believe in something new, or try to evaluate our collaborative trends objectively.

We don't dare regrets so we can be compelled to adjust. What's more, it's a job to govern, whereby deviations from predefined conditions are an abomination and a tactical offense towards the sense of self.